Horizon

SUMMER, 1964 · VOLUME VI, NUMBER 3

Flowered Hats and Siamese Cats

"Cicely Veronica is no name for an historian," said the English publisher Jonathan Cape, when, in 1935, he accepted a book by an unknown author, dealing with the English Civil War. "And particularly," he added, "it won't do for a *war* historian." Thus the owner of these frothy names, who happens also to be a great-great-great-great-grand-daughter of the renowned potter Josiah Wedgwood, became C. V. Wedgwood, historian of the many wars and peaces of the seventeenth century. Young Miss Wedgwood, who had recently finished Oxford

Wedgwood

with a First in modern history, next tackled the Thirty Years' War, probably the most complicated and difficult-to-keep-straight war in the history of Europe. The research had to be done in five languages. Miss Wedgwood already knew four of them, but learned Dutch especially for the purpose.

Not long ago, when she called at our offices to go over galleys of her article "The King's Trial" (see page 32 of this issue), we asked her how long that five-language research had taken her. "Only about four years," she said. "I don't think I'd attempt it now, but in those days I was young and reckless." The book that resulted from this recklessness is regarded by historians as the definitive book on the Thirty Years' War, and by laymen as highly readable and exciting—for Miss Wedgwood is that rare treasure, an impeccably accurate historian who, at the same time, has a novelist's feeling for character and plot, and writes about history as the rousing good story it is.

Besides publishing nearly a dozen books, all concerned with the seventeenth century, Miss Wedgwood has translated from the German *Charles V,* a biography by Carl Brandl, and *Auto da Fé,* the novel by Elias Canetti. She is a member of the Institute for Advanced Study at Princeton, gives a seminar at the University College of London, and, this year, lectured at Bryn Mawr on "Why the English Republic Failed," which is to be the subject of her next book. She is a trustee of the National Gallery, a member of the Royal Commission on Historical Manuscripts, and an active member and past-President of the English Centre of the International P.E.N. Club. When she likes, she can write next to her name "C.B.E.; Hon. LL.D.; Hon. Litt.D.; Hon. Fellow, Lady Margaret Hall, Oxford; Officer, Order of Orange-Nassau."

She lists her hobbies in *Who's Who* as poetry, drama, and window-shopping. When she called on us, she had just been pursuing the latter hobby on Fifth Avenue, and had acquired a flowery hat. It

HORIZON is published every three months by American Heritage Publishing Co., Inc.

PRESIDENT
James Parton
EDITOR-IN-CHIEF
Joseph J. Thorndike
EDITORIAL DIRECTOR, HORIZON
Oliver Jensen
EDITORIAL DIRECTOR, BOOK DIVISION
Richard M. Ketchum
ART DIRECTOR
Irwin Glusker

Editorial and executive offices: 551 Fifth Avenue, New York, N.Y. 10017.

EDITOR
Marshall B. Davidson

MANAGING EDITOR: Ralph Backlund   ASSOCIATE EDITOR: Jane Wilson
ART DIRECTOR: Elton Robinson
ASSISTANT EDITORS: Shirley Abbott, Charles L. Mee, Jr., Mary Cable, Barbara Klaw EDITORIAL ASSISTANTS: Wendy Buehr, Priscilla Flood
LIBRARIAN: Caroline Backlund
COPY EDITOR: Mary Ann Pfeiffer   *Assistant:* Joan Rehe

ADVISORY BOARD: Gilbert Highet. *Chairman,* Frederick Burkhardt, William Harlan Hale, Jotham Johnson, John Walker
EUROPEAN CONSULTING EDITOR: J. H. Plumb, *Christ's College, Cambridge*
EUROPEAN BUREAU: Gertrudis Feliu, *Chief, 11 rue du Bouloi, Paris Iᵉʳ*

Horizon

A Magazine of the Arts

SUMMER, 1964 · VOLUME VI, NUMBER 3

looked just right for a charming lady named Cicely Veronica.

Speaking of *Who's Who* and its listings, the small print under the name of Sir Compton Mackenzie takes up more than a column. In a long life—he was eighty-one on the day he sent us his article on Charles Dickens (see page 108)—he has published eighty-seven books, been knighted and decorated and showered with honorary degrees, and (to float gently back to earth) is currently President of the Croquet

Mackenzie

Association and the Siamese Cat Club. Over a period of seven years, he was President of the Dickens Fellowship, having not only the interest in Dickens that one novelist has for another but rejoicing also in personal family associations with him: Sir Compton's grandparents were in the theatre, and moved in the same eminent London circle as the great novelist, whose public readings of his novels indicated that he might well have been an actor himself.

Sir Compton interrupted work on his autobiography, which he is writing in "octaves" of eight years to a book, to write about Dickens especially for HORIZON. (Three have so far appeared in England, and he is now at work on the fourth.)

THE EDITORS

All correspondence about subscriptions should be addressed to: HORIZON Subscription Office, 379 West Center St., Marion, Ohio 43301.

Single Copies: $5.00
Subscriptions: $16.00 per year in the U.S. & Canada; elsewhere, $17.00

Annual indexes for Volumes I–V are available at $1 each. A cumulative index for Volumes I–V is available at $3. HORIZON is also indexed in the *Readers Guide to Periodical Literature.*

The editors welcome contributions but can assume no responsibility for unsolicited material.

Title registered U.S. Patent Office

Second-class postage paid at New York, N.Y., and at additional mailing offices.

COVER: This pottery statue, modeled in the exuberant style known as Remojadas, was made in Mexico between A.D. 500 and 800. It represents the goddess of childbirth and death thereby, the same deity that the Aztecs later called Cihuacoatl ("serpent-woman") and that they probably identified with the Virgin Mary after the Spaniards came. Three flat serpent heads form her headdress, and her jewelry is of shells. Her closed eyes, open mouth, and outstretched hand almost suggest sleepwalking. The statue belongs to the museum at Jalapa, Veracruz, where Lee Boltin photographed it. An article on new discoveries in Latin America begins on page 73.

SARAJEVO

Morning in Sarajevo, June 28, 1914. Archduke Franz Ferdinand (right) and Sophie, his morganatic wife, are on a round of ceremonial visits. Beside them, in a plumed hat, is General Potiorek, Governor of Bosnia. (The third plumed hat is worn by Count Harrach, the owner of the car.) Before they go much farther, the royal couple will be lying on the car seat, close to death, murdered by two shots that killed the world of the nineteenth century as well.

After fifty years of explanations, it is still difficult to see why a political murder in a remote corner of the Balkans should have set off a war that changed the world forever

The End of Innocence

A few minutes before eleven o'clock in the morning, Sunday, June 28, 1914, on the river embankment in Sarajevo, Gavrilo Princip shot the archduke Franz Ferdinand and brought a world crashing down.

After fifty years and so much pain, Sarajevo is worth a pilgrimage, but to go there is a disappointing and somehow unsettling experience: this dusty Balkan city, in its bowl of dark and barren hills, is an unlikely setting for grand tragedy. Blood and suffering are endemic to the Balkans, but Sarajevo is so mean and poor. Why should an age have died *here*? Why did the double murder of an undistinguished archduke and his morganatic wife touch off a world war, when so many graver pretexts had somehow been accommodated—or ignored—in the preceding quarter-century? It was an act that no one clearly remembers today; indeed, its details were forgotten by the time the war it engendered was six months old. Nowadays, even in Sarajevo, few pilgrims search out the place where Princip stood that morning. Nearby, on the river embankment, only a dingy little museum commemorates the lives and passions of the seven tubercular boys (of whom Princip was only one) who plotted one small blow for freedom, but who brought on a universal catastrophe. Within the museum are faded photographs, a few pitiable relics of the conspirators, a fly-specked visitors' book. A single shabby attendant guards the memorials to a political passion that seems, well, naïve to our more cynical age. "Here, in this historic place," the modest inscription runs, "Gavrilo Princip was the initiator of liberty, on the day of Saint Vitus, the 28th of June, 1914." That is all, and few visitors to present-day Yugoslavia stop to read it.

There is so much that goes unanswered, even though the facts of the case are so well known: how the failing Hapsburgs, impelled by an unlucky taste for adventure, had seized Bosnia and Herzegovina from the Turks and aggravated the racial imbalance of the Austro-Hungarian Empire; how the southern Slavs within the Empire felt themselves oppressed and increasingly demanded freedom; how the ambitious little hill kingdom of Serbia saw a chance to establish a South-Slavic hegemony over the Balkans; and how Czarist

Russia, itself near ruin, plotted with its client Serbia to turn the Austro-Hungarian southern flank. But there is so much more that needs to be taken into account: how Franz Ferdinand, the aged emperor Franz Josef's nephew, became his heir by default (Crown Prince Rudolf had committed suicide at Mayerling; Uncle Maximilian, Napoleon III's pawn, had been executed in Mexico; Franz Ferdinand's father, a pilgrim to the Holy Land, had died—most improbably—from drinking the waters of the Jordan); how the new heir—stiff, autocratic, and unapproachable, but implausibly wed in irenic middle-class marriage to the not-quite-acceptable Sophie Chotek—sensed the danger to the Empire and proposed a policy that would have given his future Slav subjects most of what they demanded; how the Serbian nationalists were driven to panic, and how the secret society of jingoes known as "The Black Hand" plotted Franz Ferdinand's death; how seven boys were recruited to do the deed, and how one of them, Gavrilo Princip, on the morning of June 28, 1914, shot Franz Ferdinand and his Sophie dead.

But why the mindlessness of the war that followed, the blundering diplomacies and reckless plans that made disaster inevitable once hostilities broke out? It is all so grotesque: great and shattering consequences without proportionate causes. When the inferno of 1914–18 ended at last, the broken survivors asked themselves the same question, seeking to comprehend the terrible thing that had happened. To have endured the inferno without a justifying reason—to be forced to admit that a war of such terror and scope had been only a blind, insouciant madness—was intolerable; it was easier to think of it as an unworthy or a wrongful cause than as a ghastly, titanic joke on history. After the event Winston Churchill wrote: "But there was a strange temper in the air. Unsatisfied by material prosperity the nations turned restlessly towards strife internal or external. . . . Almost one might think the world wished to suffer." Yet if this opinion had been widely accepted, it would have been a judgment on human nature too terrible to endure. And so a new mythology of the war grew up—a postwar mythology of materialist cynicism almost as contrived as the wartime propaganda fictions of the "Beast of

Berlin" or the wholesale slaughter of Belgian nuns. It embraced the myths of the munitions manufacturers who had plotted a war they were, in fact, helpless to control; of Machiavellian, imperialist diplomacies; of an ever-spiraling arms race, when in fact the naval race between England and Germany had, if anything, somewhat abated by 1914. But no single cause, or combination of such causes, will explain the First World War. Neither the Germans, the Austrians, the Russians, the French, the Italians, nor the British went to war to fulfill a grand ambition—to conquer Europe, or the world, or to promote an ideology. They did not even seek economic dominion through war. The somber truth is that Western civilization, for a hundred years without a major war and absorbed in a social and technological revolution—progress, in short—turned on itself in a paroxysm of slaughter.

On both sides the actual war aims, so far as they were articulated at all, were distressingly small. Merely to humiliate Serbia and to "avenge" a man whose death few particularly regretted, the Austro-Hungarian Empire began a war which cost it seven million casualties and destroyed its fabric; to prevent a senile Austria-Hungary from gaining a precarious (and inevitably short-lived) advantage in the poverty-stricken western Balkans, imperial Russia lost more than nine million men—killed, wounded, or taken prisoner. To support an ally, and to avoid the public humiliation and anxiety of canceling a mobilization order once issued, Germany lost almost two million dead, Alsace-Lorraine, a third of Poland, and its growing sphere of influence in Central Europe and the Middle East. England, to keep its word to Belgium, committed eight million men to the struggle, and lost nearly one million dead. France, to counter its German enemy and to avenge the peace treaty it had accepted in 1870, endured losses of 15 per cent of its population and initiated a process of political decline from which it may not yet have emerged.

This was the price of World War I. Two shots were fired in Sarajevo, and for more than four years thereafter half the world bled. At least ten million soldiers were killed, and twenty million were wounded or made prisoners. But the real legacy of the war was something less tangible—a quality of despair, a chaos, and a drift toward political barbarism that is with us to this day. We have not recovered yet.

In the summer of 1914 the armies marched out to Armageddon in their frogged tunics, red Zouave trousers, and gilded helmets. Five months later they were crouching in the mud, louse-ridden, half-starved, frozen, and bewildered by the enormity of it all. "Lost in the midst of two million madmen," the Frenchman Céline was to write of the war, "all of them heroes, at large and armed to the teeth! . . . sniping, plotting, flying, kneeling, digging, taking cover, wheeling, detonating, shut in on earth as in an asylum cell; intending to wreck everything in it, Germany, France, the whole world,

every breathing thing; destroying, more ferocious than a pack of mad dogs and adoring their own madness (which no dog does), a hundred, a thousand times fiercer than a thousand dogs and so infinitely more vicious! . . . Clearly it seemed to me that I had embarked on a crusade that was nothing short of an apocalypse."

The savagery of the war and the incompetence of the military commanders quickly became a commonplace. The generals proved wholly unprepared for quick-firing artillery, machine guns, field entrenchments, railroad and motor transport, and the existence of a continuous front in place of the isolated battlefield of earlier centuries. They were helpless in the face of a combat too vast, too impersonal, too technical, and too deadly to comprehend. Quite aside from their intellectual shortcomings, one is struck by the poverty of their emotional response. Kill and kill was their motto. No one in command was daunted by the bloodletting, it seems. No more imaginative battle tactic could be devised than to push strength against strength—attacking at the enemy's strongest point on the theory that one side's superior *élan* would ultimately yield up victory. Verdun in 1916 cost the French some 350,000 men and the Germans nearly as many; the German penetration was five miles, gained in a little more than three months. The Somme cost the Allies more than 600,000 casualties, the Germans almost half a million: the offensive gained a sector thirty miles wide and a maximum of seven deep in four and a half months.

That it was an insane waste of lives the combatants realized early, but no one knew what to do. The waste of honor, love, courage, and selfless devotion was the cruelest of all: at the first Battle of Ypres, in the opening days of the war, the young German schoolboy volunteers "came on like men possessed," a British historian records. They were sent in against picked battalions of British regulars who shot them to pieces on the slopes of Ypres with the trained rifle fire for which they were famous. The incident has gone down in German history as the *Kindermord von Ypern*—"the Slaughter of the Innocents at Ypres." No other phrase will do.

It was a strange world that died that summer of 1914. For ninety-nine years there had been peace in Europe: apart from the Crimean War, only eighteen months of all that time—according to Karl Polanyi—had been spent in desultory and petty European wars. Men apparently believed that peace was man's normal condition—and on those occasions when peace was momentarily broken, war was expected to be comprehensible and salutary, an ultimately useful Darwinian selection of the fittest to lead. To us, after the profuse horrors of mustard gas, trench warfare, Buchenwald, the Blitz, Coventry, and Hiroshima, to name only a few, this is incomprehensible naïveté. But that we have been disillusioned and have awaked to our condition is due to the events of 1914–18.

In the nineteenth century the belief in progress—auto-

CONTINUED ON PAGE 116

6

AFTER SARAJEVO

André Léveillé: **Mobilization in Paris,** August, 1914

Announcements of general mobilization, in August, 1914, were greeted all over Europe with enthusiasm, flag waving, and expressions of patriotic devotion. The Paris street scene shown above had its counterparts in London, Berlin, Vienna, and St. Petersburg. The artist who painted this picture noticed the shadows lengthening over the Porte St.-Denis and along the Boulevard Bonne Nouvelle, and put them in, so that they seem to loom above the excited throng. Artists, who see in terms of feeling, often note what others miss and what cannot be caught by a camera unless the photographer is an artist, too. Here, and on the following six pages, is a record of World War I as seen by artists. It forms part of an extensive collection for the forthcoming book "The American Heritage History of World War I," to be published in October, 1964. Many of these works have never been reproduced before.

Angelo Jank: **Bavarian cavalry in Galicia,** August 4, 1915

A romanticized view of the Eastern Front (left) shows well-dressed, well-organized Bavarian cavalry in Galicia, August, 1915. Of this front, Winston Churchill has said, "In its scale, in its slaughter, in the exertions of the combatants, in its military kaleidoscope, it far surpasses by magnitude and intensity all similar human episodes....Here all Central Europe tore itself to pieces and expired in agony..." The two water colors below are less romantic, perhaps because they are by artists who were also front-line soldiers. Karl Fahringer, an Austrian, painted his comrades plodding toward an Alpine front on a day of budding spring; the renowned French post-impressionist, André Dunoyer de Segonzac, who served as a sergeant of infantry, sketched French soldiers in a cemetery. Typical of life on the Western Front was the horse-drawn chow wagon. This one (opposite, near right) is American. Despite many revolutionary mechanizations, the armies of World War I were still unable to function without horses. The water-color drawing opposite at far right, showing a camouflaged trench in Lorraine, is the work of yet another sketchbook-carrying enlisted man.

Karl Fahringer: **Infantry column in the mountains**

André Dunoyer de Segonzac:
French soldiers in a cemetery near Saint-Quentin, 1917

A convoy (left) assembles for the massive French attack of April, 1917, an offensive that ended in total disaster. Its plan was fully known beforehand to the Germans through captured men and documents, and the troops, morally and physically worn out, were unequal to the demands made upon them. Mutinies followed. A far cry from the cool, collected battle scene at the top of this page is the dogged desperation of "Over the Top" (opposite), painted by John Nash late in the war. Nash, who was then regarded as an extreme "modernist," was one of several artists appointed by Lloyd George to paint the war.

Eugène Louis Veder:
Convoy before the attack in Champagne, April 12, 1917

Jean Louis Lefort:
Camouflaged trench on the Lorraine front, January 22, 1918

Henry Camus: **American field kitchen,** July, 1918

John Nash: **Over the Top**

Pierre-Bertrand: **Attack at Hartmannsweilerkopf,** 1915

Henry Farré: **Night bombing by a Peugeot,** 1917

Max von Poosch: **K.U.K. "Koros" and "Leitha" at Belgrade,** 1915

This war was a weird mixture of new and antiquated methods of destruction. Bayonet charges and countercharges took place daily. The one depicted opposite is at Hartmannsweilerkopf, in the Vosges Mountains, a summit taken and retaken so often that it became a grim joke in the official communiqués. In the shelling and capture of Belgrade, the Austrians used monitors (opposite, far left), small gunboats whose design harked back more than half a century to the American Civil War; while the use of aircraft for bombing raids was a bold step deep into the twentieth century (the painting at the bottom of the opposite page shows a Peugeot carrying out a night bombing).

The most terrifying new weapon was gas, whose first major use occurred at Ypres, in April, 1915, when the Germans released a lethal mist of chlorine that killed, disabled, or panicked hundreds of French and Canadian troops. But gas was a risky weapon; in later attacks, the wind changed, blowing it back on the attackers. At right, a Canadian has recorded the horrors of Ypres.

William P. Roberts: **Gas attack at Ypres,** 1915

Karl Sterrer: **Austrian soldiers on the Bukovina front,** 1916

To men forced to live in the filth and misery of trenches, trench making became a skill. In 1916 some Austrian troops on the stalemated Russian front in the Carpathian Mountains built a model one (above) complete with a real window, furniture, and a mascot. In 1918 John Singer Sargent was asked to tour the trenches to sketch war scenes to be preserved later in a memorial gallery. After two months, he got flu and was taken to a field hospital, where, listening to "the groans of the wounded and the chokings and coughings of gassed men," he recovered from his illness. The water color at the right shows what he saw while lying on his cot.

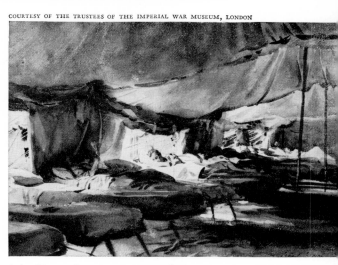

John Singer Sargent: **Interior of a hospital tent,** 1918

C.R.W. Nevinson: **The Harvest of Battle**

MUSÉE DE LA GUERRE, PARIS

Edouard Vuillard: **Interrogation of a prisoner,** 1917

Flanders Field without poppies (above) was painted in 1917 by another of the official British artists. The grisly scene shows German prisoners carrying their own and British wounded toward the rear. The interrogation of a prisoner (left) was depicted by Edouard Vuillard in 1917, when he was a member of the Home Guard. A French officer is barely seen in the foreground, while two French soldiers somberly eye the captured Boche. Though there are no corpses in Vuillard's picture, it speaks eloquently of the war-weariness and complete lack of illusion that was shared by all veterans of the trenches. The arrival of the fresh, well-equipped Americans was vital for the morale of the exhausted Allies, whatever the precise value of their contribution—which has been alternately over- and underestimated. Their military effect was not crucial until mid-1918. (The painting opposite shows American troops in Southampton.) Had the Germans been able to fight on, they would have found themselves opposed chiefly by Americans. Instead, Germany gave way, and the Americans returned to a country that, because they had gone, would never be the same again.

Sir John Lavery: **American troops at Southampton,** 1918

You will not find James Buchanan Brady, better known as Diamond Jim, in the *Dictionary of American Biography*—which is certainly the height of something or other, perhaps a virulent form of nineteenth-century academic, anti-celebrity snobbery. But the fact remains that the young man who was born, fittingly enough, the son of a free-lunch-counter (and saloon) operator, whose first job was as a hotel bellboy (he ate, characteristically, more food than he delivered), and who went on to legendary heights as a salesman of railroad equipment—and as the country's number-one eater, to even more legendary widths—left behind him an enduring name.

When aspersions were cast on the authenticity of his diamonds (his jewel collection, including a 33-carat scarfpin, cost him almost two million dollars), Jim was inclined, casually, to scratch his name with them on the doubter's windowpane. When similar skepticism was accorded his gustatory prowess, however, he did not even deign to acknowledge it. Brady, born in 1856, lived in the era of the fifteen-course dinner—and no public dancing, as we know it today, was permitted. In a sense, there was nothing to do *but* eat. And it was thus an era made to order—à la carte, of course—for Diamond Jim. Comparisons with other great gourmets ("Well," a friend once allowed, "he's a kind of combination of gourmand and gourmet") were simply preposterous. Years after he was gone, his eating feats were passed on by those who knew him. "One would be willing to match his shade," declared Albert Stevens Crockett, "against the most valiant trenchermen of all time."

For breakfast he would have a full gallon of orange juice—actually, he had several beakers of this at every meal, a fact which was later described as having prolonged his life. Then came, in rapid succession, hominy, eggs, corn bread, muffins, flapjacks, chops, fried potatoes, and a beefsteak.

This breakfast would hold him until about 11:30, at which time he would have his mid-morning snack—one which consisted of two or three dozen clams and oysters. An hour later he was ready for lunch. First, more oysters and clams, then two or three deviled crabs, next a brace of broiled lobsters, followed by a joint of beef, a salad, and several kinds of fruit pie.

During the afternoon came another snack, again a platter heaped skyward with sea-

"God, Nell, ain't it grand?"

Jim dined on Lobster,
Gorged on cake,
And died at last—
With a stummick six times
larger than normal

By CLEVELAND AMORY

DRAWING BY DAVID LEVINE

food, this time followed by several bottles of lemon soda. (Jim, the son of a saloonman, was a lifelong teetotaler.) Then, records his awed biographer Parker Morell, "after lying down for an hour or two to gather his forces together for a further assault upon the groaning board, Jim went down to dinner."

It took the late restaurateur George Rector himself to describe the rapacious repasts that Brady enjoyed for dinner. "I can affirm and testify," he said late in life, "after looking over the books of that dim era, that Diamond Jim was the best twenty-five customers we had." Rector also attested to the truth of Wilson Mizner's observations that at dinner "Jim likes his oysters sprinkled with clams" and "his sirloin steaks smothered in veal cutlets."

First, of course, came the napkin. Jim wore a napkin around his neck. But this was not due, according to Rector, "to lack of etiquette"—rather it was due "to the conformation of Mr. Brady's topography. . . . A napkin on his knee would have been as inadequate as a doily under a bass drum. Diamond Jim's stomach started at his neck and swelled out in majestic proportions, gaining power and curve as it proceeded southward. Therefore the only place where a napkin would have done him any good was around his neck. And there he wore it. It looked like a bookmark in a tome of chins."

To begin with, at dinner, came oysters. Diamond Jim would often eat as many as three dozen Lynnhaven oysters, each measuring six inches from tip to tail. ("We used to have our oysters shipped up to us from Baltimore daily," George Rector said, "and every second or third shipment would include a barrel of extra large Lynnhavens with the words 'For Mr. Brady' painted on the side of it. Even down in Maryland, the seafood dealers knew about Diamond Jim and saved all the giant oysters for him.") Then would follow half a dozen crabs, claws and all. After the crabs came a brief pause for green turtle soup—at least two portions —and then appeared what Rector described as the "deluge" of lobsters. "Six or seven giants," he said, "would suffice." Next came two portions of terrapin, two whole canvasback ducks, and, at long last, a steak and vegetables. Finally, of course, came dessert —which was supplemented by cakes and pastry. "He selected his cakes carefully— in handfuls," Rector recalled. "When he pointed at a platter of French pastry, he didn't mean any special piece of pastry. He meant the platter."

The meal would conclude with Jim ordering a two-pound box of candy which he would pass around among his guests. But if a guest actually took any, Jim made a habit of ordering another two-pound box for himself. "They make the food set better," he declared, and they evidently made the theatre set better, too. A devoted first-nighter all his life, Brady was never known to arrive at the theatre without his accompanying box of candy. And he was no mean theatre critic. "Shaw was more tolerable with bonbons," he explained, "and Ibsen was best with glacé fruit."

After the theatre, naturally, came supper —not a bird and a bottle, but several birds and several bottles, though for Jim there was never any hard liquor. Once, however, concluding a hard day's eating at Harry Hill's, the famous sporting house, he was challenged to a drinking duel by the pugilist John L. Sullivan. Over a two-hour period, Jim calmly drank some fifteen enormous steins of root beer without visible disaffect, thereby garnering the lifelong admiration of the fighter. "By God, Sir, you're a man," exclaimed Sullivan, who had been drinking Pilsener and thought Brady had been, too. "I'm proud to call you my friend! Shake hands again!"

All in all, covering a sixteen-hour, 9 A.M. to 1 A.M. span, Diamond Jim consumed a truly incredible amount of edibles. "You must be very proud of your appetite, Mr. Brady," a *grande dame* once said icily, as Brady heaved himself up from her elegant table. "And how do you ever know when your appetite is satiated?" "Why, Ma'am, "I'll tell you," Brady replied with pristine simplicity, "whenever I sit down to a meal, I always make it a point to leave just four inches between my stummick and the edge of the table. And then, when I can feel 'em rubbin' together pretty hard, I *know* I've had enough."

Most of his eating was done out. "Between Mr. Brady and the Expense Account," records Morell, "it was a case of love at first sight." And Jim, curiously, never married. For ten years he had a liaison with Edna McCaulay, a handsome blonde who had been a department-store salesgirl until Diamond Jim picked her up—only to have her, in the end, marry his best friend, Jesse Lewisohn. Ironically, before that time Lewisohn had been the lover of Jim's friend, Lillian Russell, who managed to marry four other men in between lovers but was nonetheless fated to go down in history gustatorily, if not amatorially, with Diamond Jim. For when big Lil was turning down diamonds from legions of swains, it was Diamond Jim who won her heart by teaching her new ways to eat corn on the cob.

Lillian liked her dinner ("Another pound or two, what does it matter, Jim?" she would exclaim lightheartedly) and, by that time perhaps the two foremost celebrities of the day, the pair would hold rendezvous where the chief purpose of the assignation seemed to be to see which one could assassinate the most vittles. Brady almost always won, but "for a woman, Nell done damn well." At a famous eating bout at Bustanoby's in Saratoga, however, the scales were tipped in the other direction when, before the contest, Lillian disappeared. 'I'll never forget that night," Bustanoby later said in an interview. "She slipped out to the ladies' room and came out with a heavy bundle under her arm wrapped up in a tablecloth. 'Keep this for me,' she said, 'but don't look.'" That night Lillian won fair 'n' square—what was in the tablecloth, of course, was her corset.

And Brady was, as always, a good sport. Once after an enormous evening repast at Manhattan Beach, he turned beaming to Lillian, as, happy after a Gargantuan dinner, they were watching the fireworks. "God, Nell," said Diamond Jim, "ain't it grand?"

The double standard of the day was, for Jim, no more of a problem than the women who could not, for better or worse, lure him from the pleasures of the table. There was, for example, the little matter of Stanford White's Jack Horner pie dinner, at which Jim was gustatory guest of honor, and also at which girls danced, it was alleged, "in the altogether." At this dinner a mammoth pie was placed in the center of the table and, at a given signal, each of the gentlemen present took hold of a long satin ribbon and tugged. Promptly, the sides of the pie fell apart, and a young lady clad solely in a satin arm band danced down the table to where Jim sat. All the other men cried out until altogether eleven other young ladies joined the party. Only Diamond Jim, unperturbed, went on with the business at hand.

Diamond Jim was no mean partygiver himself. In honor of his race horse Gold Heels, he once entertained fifty friends at a dinner on the roof of the Hoffman House. Between four o'clock on a Sunday afternoon and nine o'clock the following morning, more than five hundred bottles of champagne were consumed, not to mention innumerable beefsteaks and assorted delicacies. The party cost Diamond Jim more than $100,000, including $60,000 worth of baubles for the guests—diamond brooches for the ladies and diamond-studded watches for the men.

For Jim, a restaurateur would go, literally, to any lengths. There was, for instance, the case of the Fillet of Sole Marguery, à la Diamond Jim. "Diamond Jim had been

to Paris and brought home with him glad tidings of a famous dish—Fillet of Sole Marguery, prepared only at the Café de Marguery," George Rector recalled, but no restaurant in this country could duplicate the sauce. Stern measures were obviously called for. In any case George's father summoned him from Cornell, where he had been happily immersed in the study of law, and sent him to France with instructions not to return to these shores until the recipe was his, "to return either with the sauce Marguery or in it."

It took him more than a year, during which time he served as an apprentice cook, waiter, and busboy before being permitted to "get the hang of the famous sauce." At last, Rector managed "to produce a combination which was voted perfect by a jury of seven master chefs." Finally he returned to America to be met, as his ship docked in Manhattan, by an apprehensive father and a bellowing Diamond Jim. "Have you got the sauce?" Brady roared, as the gangplank lowered slowly. "I got it," young Rector screeched in reply, and that night at a private dinner at Rector's attended by Brady, Marshall Field, Victor Herbert, Sam Shubert, and several others, he made good his claim. "George," said Diamond Jim, folding his napkin over what was perhaps the widest waistcoat in the Western hemisphere, "that sole was marvelous. I've had nine helpings—and even right now, if you poured some of the sauce over a Turkish towel, I believe I could eat all of it." "He was," said George Rector, "the greatest gourmet of his time."

In the end, of course, the strain told. At fifty-six, Jim was taken to Johns Hopkins where it was discovered, under fluoroscope, that his stomach was six times as large as a normal person's. At first, when his troubles began, Jim was under the impression that he could simply order a new stomach —his preference, he said, was for that of an elephant. But when he had to settle for a new human one, he was willing, on the condition that the doctors wouldn't stop his eating. When told that he could, with care and constant diet, live ten more years, he stoutly refused. "Who wants to live ten years," he said, "if he has to do all them things? I'm gonna go on eatin' what I please as long as I can keep my food down. Then when I cash in my chips it'll be because my number's up anyway."

Five years later, on April 16, 1917, at the Shelburne Hotel in Atlantic City his number did come up.

Cleveland Amory, author of *The Proper Bostonians* and *The Last Resorts*, wrote this article for the *American Heritage Cookbook and Illustrated History of American Eating & Drinking*, published this summer.

ALBERTINA, VIENNA

*He would have been a good
artist if he had stayed at
home; he became a great one
when he brought the vigor
of the Italian Renaissance to
the fading Gothic world
of pre-Reformation Germany*

Albrecht Dürer is usually called the greatest German artist. His position may be rivaled nowadays by the rise of his immediate contemporary, Matthias Grüne-wald, whose wild and fantastic fervor is more to the modern taste than Dürer's methodical exploration of the world and man's place in it. But even if Dürer is acknowledged to be the "greatest German artist," the appellation carries for most minds an implied restriction, since to be the greatest *German* artist is to be great against competitors who are certainly fewer in number and in general less impressively considered than the artists who, not only in Dürer's century but before and after it as well, sprouted so magnificently in Italy and France.

A better introduction to Dürer is simply to say that he was a great artist, restricting that carelessly used word "great" to a handful of names from all countries and all times. Yet his Germanness is intrinsic, and a first mention of his name is somehow incomplete without reference to it. It is, however, a Ger-manness that should be dissociated from Wagnerian and post-Wagnerian ex-cesses. Mania, disorder, and violence, all of which have characterized recent German history and much recent German art, are present in Dürer's art only as devils that haunt the northern mind and must be routed by intellectual dis-cipline and spiritual purification. Dürer's two major themes are the will of God and the dignity of man—themes that not all thinkers have found compatible but that Dürer, influenced by Erasmus, could think of as identical.

In spite of his determination to build his art on a rational basis, Dürer re-mained part intellectual mystic and part mystical scientist. He studied and recorded nature as the visible expression of a double miracle, much as Leonardo da Vinci did in Italy. Leonardo was always more suave, more subtle, even a bit more guarded. He was also a more objective theorist than Dürer, who was tormented by the problem of the interrelationship between a man, his church, and his God in a way that Leonardo was able to dismiss in pondering a man's relationship to himself. But in spite of these differences, Dürer can be called a northern Leonardo (as he often is) with no more inference of second place than there would be in calling Leonardo a southern Dürer (which is never done).

Both men were as highly regarded by their contemporaries for their learning as for their achievements as artists. Both made studies of anatomy and geometry, relating them to standards of ideal beauty and to the mechanics of creating works of art. Both went outside the field of art into that of engineering. And both men, when they drew a plant or an animal, were as much botanists or zoologists as artists, not so much interested in the pattern of natural forms as in the systems of growth and construction that accounted for those patterns. Both were fascinated by human beings as natural objects, and as natural ob-jects modified by artifice: they recognized dress, coiffure, and manners not as superficies of style, but as expressions of ways of thought.

The parallels between Dürer and Leonardo could be continued and elaborated; they are the expectable evidence of exploring minds. But the similarities cease when the end results of the explorations—their applications in art—are com-pared. Leonardo's art becomes enigmatical, rather soft, often a little perverse. In some of his most elaborately studied paintings, Leonardo relinquished the world that had fascinated him as a study and yielded to the languor of escape into a more shadowy world of dream and fantasy. Although his notebooks, never meant to be seen, show us the Leonardo of universal intellect and in-satiable curiosity, his paintings are more evasive than inquiring in spirit, a private art.

Not so with Dürer. He remains absolutely decisive even when he is most complicated, and his passion is not only to inquire and to know, but to ex-pound for everybody what he has learned for himself. (His various researches were parts of a treatise on the theory of art that occupied him until the time

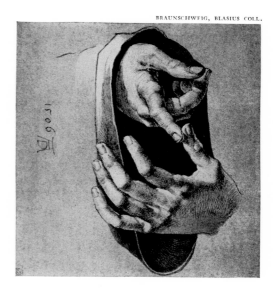

Drawings of hands abound in Dürer's work; those above are a study for the hands of the young Jesus in the painting Christ Among the Doctors *of 1506. Another lifelong pre-occupation was the self-portrait. Dürer did many, but none is more remarkable than the silverpoint drawing opposite, "made out of a mirror" in 1484 when he was only thirteen.*

Dürer's portrait of his mother (below, left) was drawn two months before she died at sixty-three, and is a remarkably objective study of an old woman whose life—as he said—had been filled with "many a painful illness, great poverty, derision, contempt, sneering words, anxieties, and other troubles." His strongest affection was reserved for his father, his first teacher and—judged by his self-portrait (below, right)—a capable draftsman himself.

Dürer's wife, by all accounts—and perhaps on the evidence of his drawing of her (above, left)—appears to have been pious, simple, and unimaginative. She was probably a nag, but he was probably a neglectful husband. He found his intellectual match in his best friend, Willibald Pirckheimer, whom Dürer portrayed as the humanist scholar he was (above, right), rather than as the rakehell he also was.

of his death.) Even when Dürer recognizes the doubts and confusions that beset us, he recognizes them with anguish rather than resignation. Art for Dürer was a vehicle that served a moral obligation imposed on the artist along with the gift of his talent—the obligation to clarify by rational examination.

Dürer was never satisfied by half-answers, nor could he permit himself the kind of answer that has been the most powerful one for many painters—the intuitive response by which the artist, as a special kind of being, transports us to a shared world that we can somehow understand through his guidance although his explanation is never explicit. Dürer is always explicit, and he is always thorough—qualities that almost by definition make a dull person and a tiresome artist, except that Dürer was as passionate by nature as he was rational by self-discipline. He was the perfect Protestant—devout, but unable to leave conventional observances unquestioned; he could accept the mystical and miraculous nature of Christianity only when the final salvation promised by faith was earned by the daily salvation that a man found in examining his own conscience. Inevitably, Dürer attached himself to the cause of Martin Luther; as an inevitable corollary, he hoped for a Protestant art as grand as the Catholic art of Italy.

This hope was not fulfilled, although Dürer came as close as any artist to pointing out where that fulfillment might lie—if only the spiritual leaders of the Reformation had been able to recognize it. They recognized instead that art contains elements of opulence and sensuousness, and held them synonymous with corruption. In this one respect Dürer might qualify for the category, so popular today, of the artist unappreciated during his lifetime. But otherwise his life was a triumphant one in spite of whatever doubts and self-goadings there were that pushed him to his realizations, and in spite of the personal calamity of a marriage wretched enough to have become famous.

He was born in Nuremberg in 1471 and died there in 1528. It was appropriate that he should die there since, in a way, he never left it, despite his fairly extensive travels. These took him throughout Germany, to the Netherlands, and especially to Italy, which for a German artist at the end of the fifteenth century was not only a matter of crossing the Alps but of crossing a century in time.

A hundred years earlier, Italian painters and sculptors had redirected the course of art while the north remained largely indifferent to the change; thus, by 1494, when Dürer made his first trip southward, the Alps not only stood between Germany and Italy but between the late Gothic style in which Dürer had been trained and a fully developed Renaissance art. Leonardo, the climactic Renaissance figure, was already in his forties when Dürer, in his early twenties, first saw Italy. The entire lifetime of Raphael—the prince of Renaissance artists, the one who summarized its classical aspirations in his Vatican frescoes—was encompassed within Dürer's birth and death dates, with generous margins at both ends. Michelangelo, whose thunderous doubts denied Raphael's serenity and marked the end of the Renaissance as a period of optimistic affirmation, was born only four years after Dürer —but between these two artists lay the whole period of discovery and change from the waning of the age of faith to the rise of the age of power.

Renaissance art had reached the northern workshops by hearsay—an echo from the humanistic circles where German artists were not ordinarily included— and by the concrete evidence of a few copies of drawings and engravings. Rough and meager as these copies were, they were strange enough to suggest to Dürer a new world on the other side of the Alps. But his first trip, which was to Venice, was a revelation beyond anything he had expected. It was more than a matter of acquainting himself with the forms of a new style: the importance of the new style was that it expressed a new attitude toward life, a new conception of the world, that could not be expressed by the forms of Gothic art.

There had been a startling change, too, in the artist's position in the social scheme—in Italy artists for the first time in history had become members of an intellectual aristocracy, the equals and companions of noblemen and popes. (Even the sculptors of ancient Greece had been regarded merely as superior artisans, since they worked with their hands, like slaves.) As members of a humanistic profession the artists of the Italian Renaissance held the position of scholars. And as men of talent they were so greatly respected as exceptional beings that Michelangelo, during his lifetime, could acquire the epithet "The Divine." But in the young Dürer's Germany the artist was still only a craftsman who might be the respected employee, but not the accepted companion, of the men he worked for. An exceptional degree of creative ability could make his work desired as a superior product, on much the same basis that gave the best carpenters the contracts for building the finest houses, but he was not expected to invent new means of expression. He applied in his own way an accepted set of conventions for pictorial descriptions and storytelling, and his conception of the world was untheoretical and rather narrow. For the northern artist, the world was a conglomeration of objects that could be reassembled as a conglomeration of standardized symbols to explain a picture's subject.

It was a formula that had been used by Flemish genius to produce magnificent expressions of mystical faith, but for Dürer it was inadequate and cramping, in an age when theoretical investigation and rational analysis were challenging the legitimacy of blind faith. Dürer's goal was to expand the expressive range of German art by bringing to it the objective disciplines of the Renaissance. He succeeded in this goal. But his greatness lay not in his achieving an Italianization of German art—fortunately this did not take place, since it might have produced only a sterile hybrid—but in the elevation and intensity that he brought to his own tradition. Nuremberg, first and last, was home.

Dürer's father was a goldsmith, and he was the third of eighteen children born, in twenty-four years, to the elder Dürer by his wife Barbara. In the tradition by which a son became apprentice to the father, young Albrecht was expected to follow the goldsmith's trade. It involved at that time more than is associated with it today: the good goldsmith was not only an artisan but a

The vistas of the Alps, and the breadth and vigor of the intellectual life to the south of them, were revelations that transformed Dürer's art after a trip to Italy in 1494. The neat little water color of a wire-drawing mill (above), painted before the trip, looked not only neat but cramped to the artist on his return; and when he painted his home city of Nuremberg circa 1496 (bottom of the page), he was able to do it with a new sweep, unity, and amplitude of vision.

For Dürer, no contrast between Italy and Germany was inconsequential. In the drawing above, he compared the bunchy complications of a Nuremberg Hausfrau's costume (left) with the more rational elegance of a Venetian lady's dress (right), from the same humanistic point of view that led him to analyze differences in styles of painting and ways of thought.

19

designer, and a designer not only of jewelry but of large and elaborate objects that might share the nature of sculpture. The trade involved skill at drawing, for the presentation of projects as well as in the chasing of designs on metal with the burin. The father had studied in the Netherlands, and Dürer later on was proud of this once-removed connection with the great Flemish painters, although he does not say which ones they were.

Dürer's father was a more than competent draftsman in the Flemish tradition, as his self-portrait on page 18 shows. But the boy Dürer, at the age of thirteen, was even better, as indicated by *his* self-portrait on page 16. (The two seem to have been a joint exercise.) The father's drawing, in comparison with the delicate and spirited work of his son, seems dry and overdetailed. The boy was already more than a craftsman: he was an artist.

In 1486 the direction of Dürer's innate capacity was recognized by his apprenticeship to a painter, Michael Wohlgemuth. Wohlgemuth was remarkable for the extremism of his version of the bunched, tortured, and exaggeratedly complicated forms of the late Gothic manner, but he was a sound craftsman. In this workshop, for more than three years, Dürer was trained in the standard techniques, including, very importantly, that of the woodcut. But under his father, Dürer had already learned the technique of the burin, through which, in the production of engravings, he was to create his finest work and to bring German art, at last, into the international front rank.

*A*fter the conclusion of his apprenticeship in 1490, Dürer traveled through the Germanic states until 1493 and then, in 1494, contracted his unhappy marriage. Agnes Frey has found defenders among Dürer scholars, who have agreed with her that she was a neglected wife, but in general the arguments have gone against her. She seems to have been a rather pretty girl, pleasant enough if not too bright, whose own disappointments in the marriage came when she discovered that her husband was not the typical solid, conventional, dependable craftsman she had expected, a man who would run a steady, prosperous shop, but a man with ambitions toward learning and culture. From her point of view, such ambitions were impractical nonsense; from Dürer's, humanistic investigation of man's spiritual nature was the goal of life.

The marriage was childless, leaving Agnes nothing but jealousy and resentment with which to fill her time, but apparently it had been a failure from the beginning. The couple were married in July, 1494; when Dürer left for his first trip to Italy that autumn, Agnes stayed behind. During their lives they took only one trip together, to the Netherlands in 1520–21, and the occasional references to his wife in Dürer's letters of that period are not flattering. The two hardly ever even ate together. But poor Agnes is even better, or worse, known because of a letter written to her after Dürer's death (but not mailed) by his best friend, the immensely learned humanist Willibald Pirckheimer, who flatly accuses her of having killed her husband by her pious nagging and by demanding that he make more and more money (a score on which he did quite well, as it was). Although we lose consciousness of it when we see Dürer only through his work, this obtrusive obbligato accompanied his entire creative life.

That life truly began with Dürer's first crossing of the Alps. The immediate effect on him can be demonstrated by the drawings on page 19, one of a wire-drawing mill done about 1489, at the end of his period of apprenticeship, and one of Nuremberg done between 1495 and 1497, after his first return from Italy. Both are landscapes where buildings and trees stretch back to a broad sky, with the curling path of a road or a river running through them. But *The Wire-drawing Mill* is conceived as a collection of individual objects defined with such individual care that they could almost have been drawn separately and

Dürer was blessed with good looks, and his self-portrait of 1498 (opposite) displays them to advantage. A bit later, in 1500, comes a self-portrait that makes a deliberate analogy to Christ the Saviour (above). And years later he posed for still another self-portrait as the Man of Sorrows (below). Yet Dürer was both modest and devout: the first portrait was painted to declare any artist's right to social, even princely, position; the portraits as Christ symbolize not vanity but the artist as a receptacle of the divine gift of genius, and man's suffering as a symbol of his union with God. The element of self is secondary.

A study from life, the nude below is even more a study of Praxitelean contrapposto, *an early (1495) example of Dürer's search for ideal proportions and the secrets of movement. Its generous proportions echo the opulence of the Venetian formulas with which Dürer had recently become acquainted.*

LOUVRE—GIRAUDON

OPPOSITE: *The technical nature of the woodcut imposes on the artist strong black-and-white contrasts and relatively thick lines, eliminating the refined detail dear to Dürer's contemporaries. But these limitations were countered by the virtues of succinctness, and Dürer capitalized on this emphatic directness to make the woodcut a fine art form.* Saint John Devours the Book *is from Dürer's version of the Apocalypse (1498), the first book designed and published by an artist as his own undertaking.*

then pasted together; one is tempted to count them, and then to count the branches in each tree and the boards in each house. This is the medieval concept of the world as a vast encyclopedia of objects, each existing in isolation except as it is found catalogued on a certain list, a sort of celestial census or inventory of the universe. Any object in the earlier Dürer landscape could be plucked out for individual examination, and the picture would be poorer only by the absence of that detail; it would not bleed, as it would if a working part had been wrenched from an organic whole.

But in the *View of Nuremberg from the West* the various trees, buildings, walls, and passages of earth are part of a scheme that has its own breadth, its own identity, its own unity. No part could be lifted out simply and cleanly; it would have to be wrenched out by violence, and would leave a wound.

Here, of course, we get into the contradiction that the inherently rational order in the second picture was imposed on an accidental landscape by the eye of the artist, which had failed to perceive such order in studying the equally accidental landscape of the earlier picture. But the contradiction that order can be found in accident is precisely what is important here: the artist's function is to reveal and interpret the world, and Dürer has not so much imposed order on the world as discovered an order already inherent in it. It is an attitude that may be echoed in the observation of any aspect of life.

Thus the drawing contrasting a lady in Venetian dress with a Nuremberg *Hausfrau* (page 19) is more than a comment on comparative fashions. Fashions are always arrived at through artifice, but the point is that the Nuremberg *Hausfrau,* with her arbitrary complications of dress, shares the taste for complexity and enumeration that produced *The Wire-drawing Mill,* while the Venetian lady's costume has the flow and harmonious unity of the later landscape. Dürer may have had no such comment in mind, but he does let the Nuremberg *Hausfrau* eye with considerable interest her Italian counterpart, as if wondering whether a shift to a new look might not be desirable; the Venetian lady, on the other hand, seems utterly confident that her own way of dress is the only reasonable one. History was on her side: the Gothic style, even in Germany, was about to be outmoded. In the five years after his return from the first Italian trip—between 1495 and 1500, from his twenty-fourth to his twenty-ninth year—Dürer set the course for a northern Renaissance.

The period includes two remarkable self-portraits, one now in the Prado (page 20), where Dürer seems to represent himself as a prince, and another in Munich (page 21), where he assumes the role of Christ. (We will see to what extent these guises were justified.) Dürer had a fondness for self-portraiture, and was quite aware that he was a handsome man. A series that begins with the self-portrait at the age of thirteen, which we have already seen, includes another drawing done about seven years later that is extraordinary in its revelation of a tense, puzzled, determined youth who must have been in the chaotic state of mind frequently characteristic of brilliant young people who are certain that a great destiny awaits them if they can only clear their way to it. The youth's questions are fully resolved in the Prado portrait: at twenty-seven Dürer was established as his own master with a degree of international fame, and he must have felt that the destiny he knew was his was really to materialize.

There is nothing relaxed in the Prado portrait, for all its studied air of casual elegance. It approaches hauteur, almost arrogance, and is saved only at the last moment from going over the edge. It is an exquisite and at the same time a forceful display of virtuosity as well as the presentation of a young man sumptuously and impeccably costumed. What is not apparent, except in historical context, is that at the turn of the sixteenth century it was also a declara-

In Dürer's mind, Nature was at once a simple fact of existence and a manifestation of God's will. He saw no contradiction between the scientific attitude that the growth and structure of plants and animals could be studied as independent phenomena and the theological dogma that gave every natural object its exact place in a divine order of things. The result of this dualism, in a study like the tempera of a columbine below, is a botanically impeccable record charged with the force of life.

OPPOSITE: *The Garden of Eden in Dürer's engraving of* The Fall of Man *is a considerable biological compendium in which each plant or animal serves a didactic symbolic purpose, at the same time that our universal parents are shown—in their final moment of innocence— as perfectly balanced and proportioned figures based on Dürer's geometrical calculations. These elements aside,* The Fall of Man *is a sumptuous harmony of the varying textures of flesh, pelts, foliage, bark, the scales of the serpent, and many other sensuous details.*

tion. The self-portrait in Dürer's time hardly existed except as an exercise using a convenient model—the artist himself—or to serve some special purpose such as the commemoration of an event. (Upon the occasion of their engagement, Dürer had painted his portrait for Agnes, and showed himself holding an eryngium, the symbol of good fortune in love and marriage.)

The Prado portrait, painted for no occasion and for no customer, but obviously as something more than an exercise, was Dürer's declaration to the world that the artist is not a workman but a gentleman. The air of hauteur hints that he is even something more—the truest of aristocrats, who owes his high position to innate qualities that he has cherished and developed rather than to the accidental fortune of having inherited a name and a position that were earned by his ancestors and merely passed on to him.

To understand this portrait from such a point of view, and yet to free it from the outrageous vanity that these ideas might carry, we must remember the predominance of allegory or symbol as the painter's language in Dürer's milieu. Although the painting is a self-likeness, it is a declaration of the position all painters should hold rather than a self-satisfied comment on the position Dürer himself was already achieving.

The allegorical premise is even more important in understanding how Dürer, a religious and reverent man, could have the audacity to do the Munich self-portrait in which he seems to assume the role of Christ. There can be no question but that the resemblance to Christ is intentional. Not only has Dürer modified his own features to bring them into an approximation of those traditionally ascribed to Christ; he has also centered the figure within the space to emphasize its hieratic effect, and has placed the hand in the position where in similar pictures of Christ it would be raised in blessing, in the tradition of Christ as the Saviour, *Salvator Mundi.* In addition to these specific references there is the permeating sacerdotal spirit of the picture overall.

Such a self-portrait today would be either an absurdity or a blasphemy. Dürer's is neither. As a quasi allegory, it is a statement of Dürer's conviction that the artist is the recipient of a gift from God, a gift that does not make an individual godlike, but at least makes him a vessel through which the will of God may be expressed. He is, in effect, a kind of priest. Thus the self-portrait as Christ is in fact conceived in humility, by which the artist accepts the divine gift and acknowledges the obligation to be worthy of it insofar as human limitations permit him to be. To Dürer's contemporaries this conception was easily apparent and would have been neither laughable nor shocking, especially since conventions of the time permitted good burghers to be portrayed among the saints as donors of altarpieces, and to be shown in attendance at such miraculous events as the Nativity.

By an odd turn the intensity of Dürer's conviction that the gift itself was divine led him away from the idea of divine inspiration. He conceived of the artist not as the vessel through whom God spoke in mystical terms—the terms of "inspiration"—but more humbly as a being who must labor through rational processes to use his gift in expounding the will of God in didactic terms. (Dürer objected to Grünewald's fervent, even hallucinatory, art as a wild growth that needed pruning.)

The Munich self-portrait, painted in 1500, comes at the moment when Dürer succeeded in harmonizing his rational-mystical philosophy, and we will see

some of its results. But in the years immediately preceding 1500, he had been engaged in the production of woodcuts, notably a series illustrating the Apocalypse, in which the swelling flood of mystical fervor seems at first to have drowned any rational approach (page 23). Saint John's hallucinatory revelations would seem, in any case, hardly appropriate subjects for cool and analytical interpretation. What Dürer did was to take familiar iconography, even drawing upon the schemes of woodcuts that had appeared in earlier German Bibles, and transform the spirit as well as the physical character of the woodcut. His large compositions, freed from their secondary function as adjuncts to a text, became independently expressive. He organized the apocalyptic vision on a pictorial and interpretative scale that, by analogy, was like the development of a familiar melody into a symphony. He opened vast earthly and heavenly panoramas in which the fantastic events are the more fantastic for the explicitly defined elaboration of their details.

The participants in this majestic and terrible drama, whether human, divine, or monstrous, are invested with life and the capacity for movement and psychological response. They are no longer merely symbols to be read, but exist with absolute conviction in themselves. Each element is so firmly knit into a unified scheme, no matter how tempestuous, that we must accept the actuality of their visionary conjunctions. As an effete device, this way of giving factual existence to fantasy has become the formula for contemporary surrealism; more solidly, Dürer was applying the power to organize energy-charged forms, which had come to him with his discovery of Mantegna. The powerful effect of visionary wildness, in the end, owes its force neither to inspiration nor to formula, but to the artist's rational control of the processes of creating and combining images into an expressive whole.

This imposition of rational control over the creative process increasingly occupied Dürer for five years after 1500—the dividing line marked by the Christ-like self-portrait. His plant and animal studies (such as the *Columbine* on page 24) may be aesthetically delightful, but they served him primarily as a form of research for the synthesis of elaborate compositions. Inevitably his determination to combine natural fact, philosophical truth, and optical delight in a single work led Dürer to formulate a set of proportions for the ideal human bodies, male and female. Such formulations, recurrent since ancient Greece and now visible in their most temporary manifestations in whatever male and female vogues are set by the movies and advertising, usually produce a male figure that remains handsome over the centuries and a female one that begins to look odd before long, since the artifices available to women for the modification of what nature intended have always been so enthusiastically applied as to stand in the way of creating an objective ideal.

This is true in Dürer's *Fall of Man* (page 25) of 1504, one of his most opulent engravings, where he delineates his ideal nudes as Adam and Eve. The Adam, on any beach today (or in the past), would be an admired figure; the Eve, with her look of having been somehow pressed downward so that she spread outward, may strike us as less successful. But this is not really the point. The point is that in an engraving of unsurpassable technical brilliance, Dürer as a Renaissance master achieved a full synthesis of the natural world in terms of the harmonious relationships of humanism.

The Fall of Man, of all Dürer's engravings, is the one that comes nearest to standing complete in its pure visual splendor alone. But so entirely superficial a production was, in a double sense, inconceivable for Dürer. Iconographically *The Fall of Man* refers to the "four humors," or "temperaments," fluids that were thought to fuse in man's nature and that were in perfect balance until

Every animal, large or small, fascinated Dürer; he had the insatiable curiosity of the naturalist. In Venice he was as absorbed by the sea creatures of the warm lagoon as by the painters of humanism. In the Netherlands he ventured into the marshes of Zeeland to look at a beached whale—thereby contracting the malaria that indubitably shortened his life. For him, a dead hooded crow, picked up in the fields and painted on parchment with the finest of brushes (below), was an equally miraculous part of the miraculous whole.

OPPOSITE: *The idea of the Christian as a warrior battling the temptations of the world goes back to Saint Paul and is still current in "Onward, Christian Soldiers." In Dürer's* engraving Knight, Death, and the Devil *the foe is impotent against the armor of virile faith; the Christian knight rides unharmed through the wilderness to the heavenly city on the hill.*

As a Christian statement, St. Jerome in His
Study (below) apotheosizes service to God
through contemplation. But at a much cozier
level this beatific, sun-filled cell is the
dream of the scholarly good life—uninter-
rupted by student papers, committee meetings,
and domestic trivia—that for generations
has seduced men into seeking professorships.

Adam succumbed to temptation. The animals in the background, which seem
to be only ornamental accessories to the Garden of Eden, symbolize these
temperaments. The elk, rabbit, cat, and ox stand respectively for the melancholic, sanguine, choleric, and phlegmatic humors; the serpent's meaning is
clear; the parrot, a symbol of wisdom, is a balancing opposite in this perfectly
balanced composition. Possibly the fact that the wise parrot's back is turned
to the serpent at this crucial moment is a lapse, and thus a comment on the
disaster that is about to occur. As for the mouse, the Dürer scholar Erwin
Panofsky points out that the artist's contemporaries "would have shared his
delight in paralleling the tense relation between Adam
and Eve to that between a mouse and a cat crouching
to spring . . ." And as Adam reaches tentatively toward
the forbidden fruit, he still grasps a mountain ash, the
tree of life.

Dürer was now internationally renowned, and in 1505,
eleven years after the first trip, he returned to Italy not
as a tourist but at a master who had brought German art
into the Renaissance current, and who had as much to
offer his fellow master-artists as he had to learn from
them. He studied Venetian colorism and became interested in the mannerist painters who, paradoxically, were
returning to somewhat Gothicized forms. But above all
he continued, during the second trip and after his return
to Nuremberg, to develop the ideas that he intended
to work up as a summary of the theory and practice of
art in the service of humanistic learning. The climactic
expression of his genius came in 1513 and 1514 with
three engravings that, although conceived as individually
independent statements, can be grouped as a trilogy
expounding the triple aspect of virtue as represented
by three ways of life. *Knight, Death, and the Devil*
(page 27) illustrates the moral virtue of Christian action; *Saint Jerome in His Study* (left) is a wonderfully
happy celebration of the theological virtue of spiritual
contemplation; and *Melencolia I* (opposite) examines
and questions the intellectual virtues of the world that
was most Dürer's own, the world of science and art.

Each engraving is built on its own complicated icono-
graphical scheme (brilliantly analyzed by Panofsky,
upon whom any discussion of Dürer must basically depend), but Dürer's genius was such that he could be
simultaneously a sort of cartographer of symbols and a
powerful, expressive artist by the less explicit, and more
demanding, standard of pure expression. The pleasure we take in a Dürer
cannot be complete unless its symbolic program is explained, but the proof of
his creative greatness is that even if these specific explanations were lost forever,
the essence of what he says would still be relayed to us powerfully and movingly.

Knight, Death, and the Devil is built on the idea of life as a journey through
dark places where the traveler is threatened with perils and temptations, a
simile so old (and already so old in Dürer's time) and so obvious that in most
treatments we can hardly meet it with anything more sympathetic than amused
tolerance. But it is impossible to look at Dürer's version without being held.
After the first recognition of the analogy, we are drawn into the complications
of a wilderness where every angle of rock and every twist of root takes its place

OPPOSITE: *In its complex interweaving of
questions, answers, and unintentional prophecy,
the engraving* Melencolia I *is Dürer's climactic work. Here he reaches back to Plato's
theory of "divine frenzy," attempts to reconcile its Christian interpretation with the
Renaissance passion for universal knowledge,
and ends by anticipating the twentieth century's most agonizing doubt: "What, when all is
said and done, can we really know and do?"*

within a mass of other details that combine pageantry with threat and mystery, phantasmagoria with lucidity. The knight and his noble horse are always firm, determined, impregnable, and unsullied, reducing Death and his pitiful nag to beggary and revealing the fearsome Devil as a mere scareface. Opposed by serene faith and virile action, the temptations of the world are only *terricula et phantasmata*—spooks and phantoms, as Erasmus calls them in his *Enchiridion*, certainly known to Dürer and perhaps the source of this conception.

In *Saint Jerome in His Study* the dark and perilous wilderness that must be braved by the man of action is replaced by the simple blessedness, the blissful privacy of a cloistered cell where the man of contemplation works at his desk. Cannily, Dürer creates impeccable order in this limited space (with its psychological extension into the spirit of ordered thought) by placing each object frontally, at right angles, or at forty-five degrees to the observer. Everything within this precise perspective contributes to its peacefulness. The lion half dozes in the light that spreads with such a gentle sparkle through the room. Even the hourglass, which in *Knight, Death, and the Devil* was brandished by Death as a threatening symbol of mortality, hangs on Saint Jerome's wall so matter of factly that one can imagine the rustle of its sands, in the quiet study, as a reassuring accompaniment to the Saint's consciousness of the presence of his eternal God.

After the forceful decisiveness of *Knight, Death, and the Devil,* and the tranquil order of *Saint Jerome in His Study,* Dürer's *Melencolia I* is puzzling, complex, and self-contradictory. Its symbolism, in a full treatise, winds its roots through all of classical, medieval, and Renaissance thought, but comes ultimately to the conclusion that genius is at once a condition of power and of helplessness, of privilege and frustration, a conclusion that Dürer had reached when, in spite of his success and his researches into the nature of art, he admitted, "what absolute beauty is, I know not. Nobody knows it except God."

In connection with *The Fall of Man* we said that the four humors, or temperaments, were thought of as having been in perfect balance before Adam succumbed. Thereafter the imbalance that gave one humor preponderance over the others determined each man's temperament—whether he was lively or stolid, subject to this or to that form of vice, gifted with one kind of talent or another or none. The melancholic humor, while it carried a capacity for art and science, also carried vulnerability to madness, sloth, and inaction.

In Dürer's engraving a large proportion of the symbols are connected with geometry, which greatly occupied him as the basis of creation. Others are connected with building and carpentry—geometry applied to a man-constructed world, as God applied it to the creation of the universe. The planet Saturn and the rainbow refer to astronomy; there are many implements of calculation and measurement. Even so small a detail as the wreath on the head of the figure of genius is significant: the leaves, which we glance at and accept as the laurel of fame, are actually those of the water ranunculus, considered a remedy for the symptoms of the melancholic humor.

In the midst of the disarray of instruments, this disorder that comes from the defeating complexity of knowledge, an infant scribbles on his slate, typifying action without thought, while the thoughtful genius is rendered impotent of action by the weight of a universe that "nobody knows except God." Dürer's statement in *Melencolia I* is too profound to be bitter, and is saved from ultimate pessimism by the recognition of a Power, a God, that exists and knows the secrets that no learning can decipher. Thus the melancholy of genius is sublime. But so extensive are the connotations and the side currents of this

30

The Four Apostles *shows St. John the Evangelist and St. Peter at the left, St. Mark and St. Paul at the right. These two panels began as the wings of what promised to be Dürer's greatest painting, a triptych that was abandoned when Nuremberg went Lutheran. Dürer then recast the two wings, offered them as "a little present" to the city, and received in return a "present" of a hundred guilders, plus twelve for his wife and two for his servant.*

personal testament, conceived four hundred and fifty years ago, that it can also be read as an anticipation of the philosophies of negation and despair on which entire schools of twentieth-century art are based.

But for Dürer negation and despair were beyond admitting. His last major work, painted in 1526, reaffirmed the unity of man, God, and cosmos, and was accompanied by an appeal to all men to observe reason and moderation on earth. The *Four Apostles* (seen at left), two tall, narrow panels originally planned as the flanking wings of a triptych, show Saint John the Evangelist and Saint Paul in the left and right foregrounds, with Saint Peter and Saint Mark (an Evangelist but not an apostle) behind them. But, again varying the theme of the four humors, Dürer makes each saint the personification of a temperament, in balanced harmony symbolizing the fourfold image of the Divine.

Saint John, young and rosy-cheeked, represents the happiest of the temperaments, the sanguine. He is dressed in the warm colors of a happy season; his posture is relaxed and assured. Saint Paul is another symbol of melancholy, the noblest humor—a less disturbed one than the genius of *Melencolia I*. His stance is reserved, majestic, but intense. Saint Peter, dominated by the phlegmatic humor, is patient, resigned, old, and wintry. Saint Mark, with rolling eyes and bared teeth, his agitation approaching frenzy, is a choleric.

For Dürer's contemporaries these identifications extended into affiliations with the four seasons, the four times of day, the four ages of man, in a system by which the number four, in its perfect balance, was the basis of a world with four points to its compass, including four races of man, watered by the four mystical rivers of Paradise. A numerical game in some of its elaborations, the concept is essentially mighty through its very simplicity, and Dürer portrayed the apostles in forms of corresponding simplicity and grandeur (one need only compare the robe of Saint Paul with that of the genius in *Melencolia I*).

To these panels Dürer added tablets quoting from the writings of the four holy messengers, inveighing against heresy and false prophecy. The quotations were preceded by Dürer's own warning against the radicals who departed from the true word of God. The reference was to the Catholic abuses that had first forced Luther away from the Catholic Church, and then to the Protestant excesses that in turn had forced him into the position of a counterrevolutionary. When the panels were moved from Protestant Nuremberg to Catholic Munich in 1627, the admonitory additions were sawed off. Recently replaced, their interest may be only historical, but they are a footnote reflecting the secular consciousness that accompanied Dürer's mystical humanism.

In 1526, when he completed the *Four Apostles* and presented them to the city of Nuremberg, Dürer was fifty-five years old and suffering from a lingering illness. Four years earlier, conscious of his shortening life, he had again served himself as model for a figure of Christ, this time showing his nude and ravaged body and anguished face as the Man of Sorrows (see page 21). To the end he identified man with God. He died on April 6, 1528.

This is the third in a series of HORIZON *articles about great artists by John Canaday, art critic of* The New York Times. *In the next issue: Thomas Eakins.*

For further reading: The Life and Art of Albrecht Dürer *by Erwin Panofsky (Princeton, 1955), the one irreplaceable book on the subject;* Complete Woodcuts of Albrecht Dürer, *edited by Willi Kurth (Dover paperback, 1963); and* A History of Engraving and Etching *by Arthur M. Hind (Dover), a reprint of a classic book on the subject that includes a good chapter on Dürer.*

The capital letters which embellish these pages are Dürer's early version of traditional German Fraktur, *from his famous treatises on proportion c. 1525.*

THE KING'S TRIAL

Kings had been killed before, had been murdered openly or in secret; but Charles I was the first ruling sovereign to be brought to trial by his own people, condemned, and—still the King—executed

By C. V. WEDGWOOD

The trial of Charles I is perhaps the most dramatic event in British history, and we know a great deal about it from eye and ear witnesses. Defeated in a civil war, the King was brought to trial by an armed minority of his subjects, arraigned as a "tyrant, traitor, and murderer," sentenced to death, and beheaded in January, 1649.

The Regicides, of whom Oliver Cromwell is the most famous, tried the King with maximum publicity in Westminster Hall because they gloried in their deed. This element of showmanship and its effect on the reporting of the trial first stimulated me to make a full study of the contemporary records.

What arrangements were made for reporting the trial? Were Cromwell and his associates alive to the problem of public relations? They wanted the trial widely reported—how did they arrange it? And was their effort successful?

Newspapers were in their infancy, but they existed, and the party in power had already established a censorship. Nine officially licensed newspapers carried reports of the trial, some of them verbatim. Two papers even published special supplements devoted to the trial alone.

The variations between the verbatim texts are slight. A manuscript report subsequently corrected and passed by the presiding judge (John Bradshaw) has only very minor differences. I conclude therefore that all reporting of the speeches probably stems from a single authorized text, made up by collating the shorthand notes of a number of clerks in different parts of the Court and passed by the official censor. But the newspaper accounts have touches of color and description which vary from paper to paper, no doubt indicating that different editors in the Hall had different personal reactions.

After the King's death, the fullest press account was reissued to meet public demand. I have found versions of it translated and issued in France, Germany, the Low Countries, Italy, and Poland. But before the end of the year, further printing of this or any account *in England* was forbidden.

The reason? I believe that the republican government had miscalculated the effect. Convinced that they were right in what they did, they forgot how easily public sympathy is aroused by the sight of a man courageously facing the worst. And Charles was no fool either—he had said many things during his trial which impugned the legal position of the new government. Publication of the text of the trial was thus, belatedly, seen to be dangerous.

It has often been asserted by Royalists that the text of the trial omits much of what the King said. After meticulous examination of the printed and manuscript sources, I feel sure that this is not so. The King's words, as reported, are so effective a statement of his case, and so sharp an attack on his accusers, that there has clearly been no censorship. Those in charge of the proceedings were too proud to garble his words: they believed him to be a wicked man who would condemn himself out of his own mouth, and did not realize that he made a quite different effect.

But there was censorship of a different kind in the licensed reports, designed to conceal the disunity in their own ranks. Thus a hysterical plea for adjournment from one of the judges is not reported. And when Lady Fairfax, wife of Cromwell's own Commander in Chief, called out "Oliver Cromwell is a traitor," no journalist mentioned it.

How, then, do we know about these and other incidents? Because, eleven years later, the surviving members of the Court were tried for treason after the Restoration of Charles II. Witnesses then came forward with all manner of details, some credible, some not.

We thus have two kinds of evidence about the trial of King Charles—the immediate contemporary reports, and the things remembered eleven years later. This presents a fascinating problem of evidence, for if neither kind of evidence is absolutely reliable in every point, both contain much that is vivid and has the stamp of truth. By carefully comparing the two kinds, and by assembling all other contemporary references to the trial, I believe I have reconstructed the trial, as accurately as possible, word by word and minute by minute.

The King Seated at His Trial, *by an obscure artist named Edward Bower, is the last known painting of Charles I.*

The King's trial began on Saturday, January 20, 1648. In the morning of that bitter-cold day, Charles was taken from his closely guarded chamber at St. James's Palace and brought to a private house belonging to Sir Robert Cotton, on the Thames near Westminster Hall where the trial was to be held. Colonel Tomlinson, who was responsible for his safety and took no avoidable risk, had him conveyed in a closed sedan chair. He was surrounded on all sides by foot soldiers marching in close formation. He could neither be seen nor approached. Tomlinson avoided as far as possible narrow or built-up places where an obstruction or an ambush might facilitate a rescue. The King was carried across the park from St. James's into the rambling precincts of his palace of Whitehall, and straight to the river at the garden stairs where a curtained barge awaited him. An old palace servant, John Henry, a Welshman, lived in the house adjoining the stairs and had charge of them. He was at his door, with his seventeen-year-old son, to watch the King go by, and as he walked from his chair to the barge, the only daylight moment of his journey, Charles called a friendly recognition: "Art thou alive yet?"

He was carried up the Thames for half a mile, beyond the usual landing place for Westminster Hall, as far as the private landing place of Cotton House. All the way along the banks, boats filled with curious spectators watched his covered barge go by, preceded and followed by Colonel Tomlinson's troops, closely packed in open boats. Disembarking, he walked between rows of soldiers across the frost-bound garden into the well-secured and well-appointed house which was to be his prison during the trial.

By two in the afternoon, spectators had filled the lower part of Westminster Hall. The galleries directly above the judges' seats were crammed, and some enterprising people had scrambled up into the embrasures of the high Gothic windows. Outside, on the leads, soldiers were on guard; otherwise the inquisitive would have clambered onto the sloping roofs below the windows and broken the thick glazed panes to see into the Hall.

The faith of Cromwell and the Regicides in their cause was reflected in the decision to hold the trial in public; their underlying fears found expression in the arrangement by which the proceedings were sited at the west end of the Hall so that the greater part of the audience would see little and hear less.

By an Act of the House of Commons, a High Court of Justice consisting of one hundred and thirty-five Commissioners had been called into being for the space of one month to try the King. One hundred and thirty-five men had been named to serve as

Commissioners of this special court, but since not all had been asked whether they wished to serve, a wide margin had been allowed for absentees, and the quorum had been fixed at twenty. As it turned out, the number of Commissioners to appear varied from day to day; there were never fewer than fifty-four nor more than seventy-one. At the beginning of the trial, sixty-eight Commissioners appeared in the Hall, preceded by twenty halberdiers and by officers solemnly carrying the sword and mace, the rear brought up by a further party of guards. They took their places on the tiered benches covered with red baize that had been set up for them below the great south window. The chair reserved for the Lord President, John Bradshaw, was somewhat raised in the middle of the front row. He had a reading desk and scarlet cushion in front of him.

Phelps, one of the clerks, now rose to his feet and read out the preamble of the Commission empowering the Court to act. Bradshaw then ordered the prisoner to be brought, and twelve of the halberdiers marched off to fetch him.

While the King was on his way, Phelps read the roll call, the Commissioners who were present rising to their names. As he called on Lord Fairfax,* a masked lady in one of the nearer galleries briefly raised her voice in protest, though her words were hardly intelligible. Later it would be said that she had cried out: "He has more wit than to be here," or, at somewhat greater length, that "the Lord Fairfax was not there in person, that he never would sit among them and they did him wrong to name him."

Now the King himself appeared, preceded and followed by soldiers who took up their stations on either side of the Court. He was dressed in black, wearing round his neck his blue ribbon and jeweled George, and on his black cloak the great irradiating silver star of the Garter. He walked quickly without looking to right or left and sat down in a red velvet chair that had been set for him. He now had his back to the people gathered in the Hall. All that any of them could see was his tall black hat, and his gray hair falling onto his shoulders. Only those in the galleries had any view of his face. He was impassive, showing no flicker of recognition or curiosity.

There cannot have been silence in that enormous, crowded room. Yet above the shuffling, the rustling murmur, the breathing, the coughing, the footfalls, there must have been in the railed-off enclosure where the King faced his judges, a moment of tenseness, of at least a limited silence, before Bradshaw began: "Charles Stuart, King of England," he said, "the Commons of England, assembled in Parliament, being sensi-

This scene of the King's trial illustrates a book by one Dr. John Nalson, published after the Restoration. Charles, with his back to the public, sits opposite his judges. Commenting that His Majesty wore his hat during the trial, Nalson says, "they, who thought it not Manners to take off his Hat, yet thought it no Sin to take off His Sacred Head."

* Thomas, Lord Fairfax was the commander-in-chief of the army which had defeated the King; Oliver Cromwell was general of the cavalry. Fairfax, though a good soldier, had no political judgment; he disapproved of the King's trial but did nothing to hold back Cromwell and the fanatics.

ble of the great calamities that have been brought upon this nation, and of the innocent blood that hath been shed in this nation, which are referred to you as the author of it; and according to that duty which they owe to God, to the Nation, and to themselves; and according to that power and fundamental trust that is reposed in them by the people, have constituted this High Court of Justice before which you are now brought, and you are to hear your charge upon which the Court will proceed."

He stopped, and one of the prosecutors, John Cook, instantly followed on his cue: "My Lord, in behalf of the Commons of England, and of all the people thereof, I do accuse"—and here he swung round and glared at the prisoner—"Charles Stuart here present, of high treason, and high misdemeanors, and I do, in the name of the Commons of England, desire the charge may be read unto him."

He had it in his hand, the heavy scroll of parchment, half unrolled.

"Hold a little," said the King, but Cook continued to unroll the indictment. Charles lifted the silver-headed cane that he habitually carried and tapped Cook two or three times on the arm to attract his attention; Cook did not turn but the head of the cane fell off. There was no one near enough to retrieve it, and the King, after a second's pause, stooped for it himself.

"Sir," said Bradshaw, "the Court commands the charge to be read; if you have anything to say afterward, you may be heard."

Charles remained silent, and Cook launched into the charge with evident enjoyment. It was the first time that the King knew precisely what the accusation was. He must have listened attentively, though he acted a contemptuous indifference.

In its final form the charge was of no overwhelming length. It would have taken less than ten minutes to read, and it went direct to the heart of the matter. As King of England, Charles had been "trusted with a limited power, to govern by, and according to the laws of the land, and not otherwise . . ." He had, however, conceived "a wicked design to erect and uphold in himself an unlimited tyrannical power to rule according to his will, and to overthrow the rights and liberties of the people . . ." In pursuit of this design he had "traitorously and maliciously levied war against the present Parliament, and the people therein represented." After this accusation came a list of those places at which the King had been present at the head of his troops during the first civil war. Next he was accused of endeavoring to gain help for his designs by

procuring "invasions from foreign parts." Then, after his defeat, he had "renewed, or caused to be renewed, the said war against the Parliament, and good people of this nation, in this present year . . ." and given commissions to his son and to others to do so. He was thus responsible for "all the treasons, murders, rapines, burnings, spoils, desolations, damage and mischief to this nation, acted or committed in the said wars, or occasioned thereby." For these reasons, Cook concluded, on behalf of the people of England, he impeached "the said Charles Stuart, as a Tyrant, Traitor, Murderer, and a public and implacable Enemy to the Commonwealth of England . . ."

During the reading the King had looked up at the galleries, scanned the faces of the Commissioners, and turned about to take stock of the crowd behind him in the Hall. His countenance betrayed no emotion at all until Cook pronounced the words "tyrant, traitor and murderer" whereupon "he laughed as he sat, in the face of the Court."

Cook had done, and now Bradshaw faced the haughty prisoner with the first and vital question. "Sir, you have now heard your charge . . . the Court expects your answer."

The King had never, in the whole course of his life, been a good speaker. He had a reasonably quick wit, but it was notorious that he had a speech impediment. However, the intensity of the moment worked on the King with the incalculable power of shock, and he was, for the first and last time in his life, fluent, strong, and clear.

"I would know by what power I am called hither," he began, with cold amazement, "I would know by what authority, I mean *lawful*." He emphasized the word and threw in scornfully: "There are many unlawful authorities in the world; thieves and robbers by the highways . . . I have a trust committed to me by God, by old and lawful descent; I will not betray it, to answer a new unlawful authority; therefore resolve me that, and you shall hear more of me."

Bradshaw somewhat irritably exhorted the King to answer "in the name of the people of England, of which you are *elected* King."

This was altogether too wide of the facts, and Charles came back with conviction: "England was never an elective Kingdom, but an hereditary Kingdom, for near these thousand years. . . . I do stand more for the liberty of my people than any here that come to be my pretended judges . . ."

Bradshaw, thwarted by these quick and pregnant replies, decided that the moment had come to admonish the King. "Your way of answer is to interrogate the Court, which beseems not you in this condition. You have been told of it twice or thrice."

But nothing would stop the King. He went

serenely on: "I do not come here as submitting to the Court . . . Let me see a legal authority warranted by the Word of God, the Scriptures, or warranted by the constitutions of the Kingdom, and I will answer."

To stop this continued and all-too-eloquent defiance, Bradshaw decided to cut short the proceedings and ordered the King to be removed. The words were a cue for a demonstration which had evidently been planned in advance, and some of the soldiers in the body of the Hall began to cry out "Justice! Justice!" The King was momentarily startled by the sudden shouts behind him and turned to look around. Bradshaw took this for a weakening of his resolve, and with a sudden change of tactics again asked if he would answer the charge.

Charles recovered himself at once, and as the shouting subsided, began another lengthy speech. Bradshaw could not, for some sentences, break into his discourse, and was not altogether successful when he did so. The Court would adjourn, he declared, until Monday when they would expect the King's answer. As for their right to try him, "we are satisfied with our authority."

"You have shown no lawful authority to satisfy any reasonable man," said the King, and Bradshaw was ill-advised enough to snap back at him: "That is in your apprehension; we are satisfied that are your judges."

" 'Tis not my apprehension, nor yours neither, that ought to decide it," said the King. This time Bradshaw desisted from further argument and ordered the removal of the prisoner.

On all sides of him as he left the Hall, the soldiers broke out with their cries of "Justice! Justice!" which were taken up by some of the spectators, but others shouted "God save the King." Charles went back to his room in Cotton House. The rest of the evening he spent in thinking over the events of the afternoon and writing out with a fine mixture of clarity and passion his reasons for refusing to admit the authority of the Court. Somewhat to the embarrassment of his captors, he refused to take off his clothes or go to bed that night because of the soldiers in the room. The next day, being Sunday, was wholly given over to prayer and meditation with Juxon, his chaplain.

John Cook, going home in the winter darkness, was stopped by an acquaintance who, with lugubrious curiosity, began: "I hear you are up to the ears in this business."

"I am serving the people," said Cook with dignity.

"There's a thousand to one will not give you thanks," answered his neighbor. But Cook was not to be put down. "He must die," he said, "and monarchy must die with him."

On Monday morning the Commissioners (sixty-two this time) met in private session in the Painted Chamber to consider what should be done now that they understood the King's intention of refusing to acknowledge the Court. For this was the insoluble problem which they had set themselves: to reconcile their wholly unprecedented action with the English Common Law, a law rooted in the practice and precedents of centuries.

They might have done better to assert, even to boast of, the novelty of their procedure. In that case Bradshaw could have elucidated their intentions in the most stirring language at his command instead of trying in vain to proceed correctly according to the Common Law, which was evidently not applicable. But this would have been foreign to his own conceptions and those of his colleagues; they were determined to act as though there was nothing irregular in their conduct.

If the prisoner would not plead, in a case of treason, the law laid down that he should be treated as though he had pleaded guilty. But they had wanted to demonstrate the King's guilt by calling witnesses, and allowing John Cook to condemn Charles's policies and his conduct in a stirring speech for the prosecution. Therefore the silence of the King destroyed a principal purpose of the trial. Certainly he could be taken as guilty and sentenced to death; but he could not be *proved* guilty for all the world to see.

What were they to do?

After long discussion, they decided to hold at least two more sessions, on Monday and Tuesday afternoon. If Charles continued in his refusal to plead, he would be treated as guilty and summoned before them once more, on Wednesday, to receive sentence. Execution would follow on Friday or Saturday, and the whole painful and dangerous business would be over before the end of the week.

On Monday afternoon, therefore, they proceeded to Westminster Hall and sent for the prisoner. This time seventy Commissioners were present, and the proceedings opened with a proclamation that anyone who caused a disturbance would be instantly arrested. The session was noticeably quieter than the first one.

Charles had not persisted in his refusal to go to bed. He had slept on Sunday night in spite of the soldiers, and he entered the Hall this Monday afternoon with his usual dignity, taking his seat once again in the crimson velvet chair. He saw Bradshaw look toward Cook to open the session. Charles found no reason why he should be kept waiting. This time he did not—as he had done before—tap Cook lightly on the wing of his gown; he gave him a sharp admonitory poke with his

cane. Cook swung round, furious, glared at him, then caught Bradshaw's eye and began a speech that put the cards on the table. If the King did not plead, he would be regarded as having admitted his guilt. Bradshaw now followed with an emphatic but still wholly unconvincing statement that the Court was "fully satisfied with their own authority" and that the kingdom, the King included, must therefore be satisfied with it too.

The King had now heard one threatening speech and one feeble one. He struck in, as cool and fluent as on the first day, but even more deadly, for he knew more exactly the weaknesses of his opponents and he had cleared his mind by writing out his ideas on paper. However, he did not speak from notes. Bradshaw interrupted him, but Charles was not to be bullied. He knew not only his inalienable rights as a king but also his rights as an Englishman.

"Sir, by your favor," he said, with ironical courtesy, "I know as much law as any gentleman in England; and therefore (under favor) I do plead for the liberties of the people of England more than you do: and therefore if I should impose a belief upon any man without reasons given for it, it were unreasonable."

Bradshaw found his voice again to interrupt. "Sir . . . you speak of law and reason; it is fit there should be law and reason, and there is both against you." They were not against him, as Bradshaw must have been uncomfortably aware. What was against the King was his own abuse of law in the past, his appeal seven years ago not to reason but to arms. But this case could never be proved if he would not answer the charge. "Sir, you are not to dispute our authority," commanded Bradshaw. "Sir, it will be taken notice of, that you stand in contempt of the Court, and your contempt will be recorded accordingly." No one, he blustered, would be permitted to question the capacity of *this* Court. "They sit here by the authority of the Commons of England, and all your predecessors, and you are responsible to them."

That the sovereign was responsible to the Commons, not the Commons to the sovereign, was a doctrine that none of the King's predecessors would have recognized. He was onto it at once: "show me one precedent."

Bradshaw was incensed: "Sir, you ought not to interrupt while the Court is speaking to you . . ." But the King was not to be silenced. He certainly knew as much law as any gentleman in England and more than most.

"The Commons of England was never a Court of Judicature," he said. "I would

know how they came to be so."

It was a very palpable hit. Parliament was indeed a court, but not the House of Commons. Bradshaw in desperation ordered the clerk to call on the prisoner to answer the charge.

If he hoped this formality would divert the flow of the King's eloquence, he was wrong. He merely took up his refrain: "I will answer the same, as soon as I know by what authority you do this."

Bradshaw could only bring the session to a close by ordering the guards to remove the King. But he was not to solve his problem so easily, for Charles would not go. "I do require that I may give in my reasons why I do not answer, and give me time for that."

"Sir, 'tis not for prisoners to require," Bradshaw reproved him.

"Sir," said the King, "I am not an ordinary prisoner."

They stopped short of violence; the soldiers did not surround and forcibly remove him. So he spoke on, demanding that they should listen to his reasons. "Show me that jurisdiction where reason is not to be heard," he challenged them.

Bradshaw lost his head and his temper. "We show it you here," he exploded, "the Commons of England." Then, realizing he had slipped, he hurried on to inform the King that the next session would be the final one.

Charles still did not rise to go. "Well, sir," he said, "remember that the King is not suffered to give his reasons for the liberty and freedom of all his subjects."

At last Bradshaw saw the opportunity for a rejoinder: "How great a friend you have been to the laws and liberties of the people, let all England and the world judge!" The King was shaken, or it may be that the guards were closing in, and the necessity for speed made his speech for the first time hesitant: "Sir, under favor," he began, "it was the liberty, freedom, and laws of the subject, that ever I took—defended myself with arms—I never took up arms against the people, but for the laws."

In this uncertain fashion the second day ended and the King left the Hall, to the usual shouts of "Justice." But in the narrow corridors between the Hall and Cotton House—so Thomas Herbert, the King's gentleman-in-attendance, wrote in his memoirs —one of the soldiers on guard said aloud as he passed, "God bless you, Sir." The King thanked him, but his officer struck him on the head with his cane. "The punishment exceeds the offense," said the King. The incident evidently impressed him, for he told Herbert afterward that he was sure the soldiers bore him no malice; they cried out for "Justice" because they had been ordered to

"England's Miraculous Preservation, Emblematically Described, Erected for a Perpetual Monument to Posterity" is the high-sounding title of this political cartoon of 1647. Charles, his Queen, and their Royalist supporters are floundering in the sea, while "England's ark," the House of Lords, the House of Commons, and the Westminster Assembly, are represented as "preserved and almost safe at land." The medallions represent some of the Roundhead generals. This rather enigmatic cartoon may have been intended as a plea for unity.

do so, and would do the same for their own leaders when the occasion arose.

The illusion was consoling to the King, but it was an illusion. Some of the soldiers were indeed deserters or renegades from his own army, but may not have loved him any better for that. Some were good-natured, decent men who felt a natural pity when they saw him in distress, and a respect for the dignity and calm with which he met his ordeal. But the majority of the soldiers hated him, for making war on his people, for trying to bring in foreign troops, or even the wild Irish; hated him for abandoning the Protestant cause in Europe, for persecuting godly ministers in England, for favoring papists and encouraging the friends of his French popish wife.

More crudely, many of them hated him simply for being a king with soft white hands, fine linen, and a velvet cloak who had ordered his poor subjects to be shot and cut down in battle, who had had prisoners beaten and starved, and had condemned honest John Lilburne to be whipped at the cart's tail.

Next day, Tuesday, January 23, the session in Westminster Hall began in the early afternoon. Seventy-one Commissioners were present, the largest attendance so far. The King came in with his habitual calm, looked for a moment at his judges, and sat down in his chair. Once again Cook opened the proceedings by recapitulating the charge. Then Bradshaw addressed himself to Charles. He had informed him "over and over again," he said, in the manner of a schoolmaster reasoning with a willful pupil, "that the Court did affirm their own jurisdiction; that it was not

for you, nor any other man, to dispute the jurisdiction of the supreme and highest authority of England." The Court, he must understand, would not be trifled with, and they might very well assert their authority by sentencing him out of hand. They would, however, allow him one more chance "to give your positive and final answer in plain English, whether you be guilty or not guilty of these treasons laid to your charge."

He concluded, and for a moment there was silence in the Court. When the King spoke, it was with greater deliberation than on the two previous days: "For me to acknowledge a new Court that I never heard of before, I that am your King, that should be an example to all the people of England, for to uphold justice, to maintain the old laws; indeed I do not know how to do it." He went on once again to offer to give his reasons for refusing to acknowledge them, and again Bradshaw interrupted, but the King would not be silenced.

"By your favor, you ought not to interrupt me. How I came here, I know not; there's no law for it to make your King your prisoner."

Once or twice Bradshaw tried to force his way in, before he at length stopped the King's flow of words by calling in the clerk to read out once more, and for the last time, the formal demand for the King's answer.

"Clerk, do your duty," said Bradshaw.

"Duty, Sir!" said the King, with ringing scorn.

Broughton hurriedly read out the words, requiring "Charles Stuart, King of England" to give his positive answer "by way of con-

fession or denial of the charge," and Charles, for his only response, again denied the legality of the Court.

Bradshaw, for the first time, saw an opportunity for counterattack.

"How far you have preserved the privileges of the people, your actions have spoke it," he said, "but truly, Sir, men's intentions ought to be known by their actions; you have written your meaning in bloody characters throughout the whole Kingdom . . ."

Charles did not flinch before the onslaught, which meant nothing to him since he did not think it true. He made one more attempt to speak, but was again prevented by Bradshaw.

"Sir, you have heard the pleasure of the Court, and you are (notwithstanding you will not understand it) to find that you are before a court of justice."

"I see I am before a power," said the King drily, and rose to go.

Something of a disturbance must by now have occurred, though none of the journalists ventured to describe it. But several of them reported without explanation that the Crier loudly called out "God bless the Kingdom of England!" This unprecedented shout may well have been prompted by the need to drown, or to disguise, shouts less welcome to the ears of the Commissioners, shouts of "God save the King" or "God bless you, Sir," as the King walked away between his guards.

The Commissioners, who had hitherto separated at the end of each session, now went together to the Painted Chamber. The situation was critical. The progress of the trial was little short of disastrous, and only a few fanatics (of whom John Cook was one) can have seen it in any other way. They had been prepared for the King's refusal to recognize them. But they had not been prepared for his persistence, nor for his claim to stand for the laws and liberties of his people, still less for his eloquence, for the way in which, by the authority of his presence and his words, he dominated the proceedings.

That evening in the Painted Chamber the final session was postponed, and next morning, Wednesday, the Commissioners appointed a committee to hear the witnesses. By this process they hoped to satisfy the waverers in their midst—of whom there were now many—and to indicate to the public that they did not lack evidence for the charge against the King. Several citizens of Nottingham had been found to give evidence about the King's setting up his standard at the beginning of the war; one of them was the painter who had painted the standard pole. Other witnesses were veterans who had fought through the war. Richard Blomfield, a London weaver who had been in the army of the Earl of Essex when it surrendered to the King at Fowey, gave evidence that he had seen his comrades plundered in the presence of the King contrary to the articles of surrender. Another, a husbandman from Rutlandshire, swore that at the capture of Leicester the King had not only permitted the prisoners to be stripped and cut about by his men, but when a Royalist officer had tried to stop this barbarity, had said: "I do not care if they cut them three times more, for they are mine enemies," the King saying all this while "on horseback, in bright armor, in the said town of Leicester."

One civilian witness, Henry Gooch, gave evidence that he had communicated privately with the King in the Isle of Wight during the Newport Treaty, and had received instructions to get in touch with the Prince of Wales about authorizing the raising of troops. Little is known to indicate whether Gooch was a Royalist who had been frightened into making these admissions or an *agent provocateur;* but what he said was borne out by some of the King's private correspondence intercepted during the treaty, and this was also exhibited as evidence.

The depositions of the witnesses were not very impressive, but they put beyond doubt the King's personal participation in the war and his intention of continuing it, even during the treaty negotiations. They may have helped a little to strengthen the wavering resolution of the more doubtful Regicides. At any rate some of the newspapers printed the evidence in whole or in part.

It had been earlier asserted that every

sovereign in Europe would hasten to the help of King Charles as soon as his life was threatened. But by this time even the Royalists had ceased to believe this. Once, it had been confidently stated that the Queen of Sweden was preparing an army of ten thousand in "fourteen tall ships," with equivalent help from France and Holland. But the story was taller than the ships, and no more had been heard of them. The only hope on the Royalist horizon came from the King's nephew, Prince Rupert. After commanding the Royalist cavalry in the war, he had gone abroad and linked his fortunes to those of the Prince of Wales in Holland. Here he had been given command of half a dozen ships, revolted from the English fleet, in poor condition and with mutinous crews. Displaying his usual resourcefulness and energy, he had restored order in the ships and, by a little well-thought-out piracy in the Narrow Seas, had increased their number. About this time his fleet had left the shelter of the Dutch coast, fourteen sail in all, "bending toward Ireland, driving the whole Channel before them." But there was no way that he could give direct help to the King; a landing was out of the question.

The King of France—or rather his regents—when the trial was first foreshadowed, had issued a manifesto denouncing the murderous rebels of England, but since then a revolt in Paris had caused the Queen regent to flee from the capital with the child King. The French government was in no condition to make any further gesture. According to the English newspapers the rebels of the Paris *Parlement* had set up their banners, inscribed *Salus populi suprema lex,* in the heart of the capital. They had at all events taken control, and Paris, besieged by the royal forces, was cut off from news and supplies from the outer world. It was bitterly cold, and firewood was almost unprocurable. The exiled Queen of England, in the half-deserted Louvre, waited for news of her husband in numb despair.

In Holland the Prince of Wales, coming in person to the meeting of the Dutch Estates at The Hague, implored them to send help to his father. They responded after a fashion; two envoys were despatched, who actually arrived in England late in January bearing a solemn appeal from the Dutch to delay the trial of the King and submit the whole matter to arbitration.

But the formalities of diplomacy would take time, and while the Dutch envoys were being formally received at Gravesend, the Court of Justice had come to a final decision. After hearing the witnesses on January 25, the forty-six Commissioners present (it was the smallest attendance yet recorded)

resolved that they could now proceed to sentence the King to death. There was some discussion of the propriety of deposing him first, but this was in the end passed over, and a small subcommittee was appointed to draw up the sentence. Cromwell was not on this committee, which consisted of only seven members.

Next day, January 26, when the Commissioners reassembled in the afternoon, sixty-two were present, a slight improvement on the very poor attendance of the previous day. The draft sentence was produced, condemning the King as "a tyrant, traitor, murderer and a public enemy to be put to death by the severing of his head from his body." The public were not admitted to the discussions, which continued throughout the afternoon.

When the last session of the trial opened, it was known to most of those present, and certainly to the prisoner, that the purpose of the Court was to pass sentence. To indicate the solemnity of the occasion, Bradshaw was, for the first time, robed in red. As the King came in, the soldiers and some of the spectators shouted for Justice! and Execution! Charles was calm and purposeful. Instead of waiting until the Lord President opened the proceedings, he began at once: "I shall desire a word to be heard a little, and I hope I shall give no occasion of interruption."

Bradshaw was taken aback, but was determined that the prisoner should not be allowed to make the opening speech; there was a brief tussle before the King gave way, on the understanding that he would be heard later, and Bradshaw addressed the Court: "Gentlemen, it is well known to all or most of you here present, that the prisoner at the bar hath been several times convented and brought before this Court to make answer to a charge of treason, and other high crimes exhibited against him in the name of the people of England . . ."

At this moment there was a stir in one of the galleries where two masked ladies sat side by side, and one of them called out: "Not half, not a quarter of the people of England. Oliver Cromwell is a traitor." Colonel Axtell, who was in charge of security in the Hall, ordered his men to level their muskets at her. Some said that they heard him shout "Down with the whores." Her companions in the gallery were as anxious to silence her as Colonel Axtell was, and within seconds she was hustled out, and Bradshaw resumed his interrupted speech.

Not very many people can have heard the exact words which had been hurled at the heads of Bradshaw and Cromwell, though there was, of course, no doubt of their general bearing. The identity of the speaker was

Of the fifty-nine signers of the death warrant, forty-one were still living when the monarchy was restored in 1660. Three succeeded in fleeing to New England and twelve to Europe, where they lived out their days. The rest were brought to trial. Of these, nine were hanged, drawn, and quartered, while the less important or more repentant were sentenced to life imprisonment. Cromwell, Bradshaw, and Ireton had died; their bodies were dragged from tombs in Westminster Abbey, exposed, and beheaded.

even more obscure; it was unknown to the man who had sold her the seat, and her face was visible to no one. Colonel Axtell cannot have recognized her, and the newspapers briefly commented on the interruption of a "malignant lady." But the masked interrupter was Lady Fairfax, who had come, accompanied by a friend, to relieve her conscience, and perhaps also to relieve her husband's. The caution with which she concealed her identity suggests that this strong-minded lady was acting without her husband's knowledge.

As the noise subsided, Bradshaw had continued speaking. The Court, he said, had fully considered the case: the prisoner, having refused to plead, could be regarded as having confessed. Furthermore, the things with which he was charged were notorious. They had therefore agreed upon the sentence, but were none the less willing to hear him speak.

Charles now made an eloquent plea for a hearing before the Lords and Commons. Bradshaw could only reiterate that the King had already delayed justice for many days by refusing to plead, and ought not to be permitted to delay it any further, but as he warmed to his ungrateful task, he was aware of a barely suppressed disturbance among the Commissioners on his left.

It was the excitable John Downes. His neighbors to the right and left were resolute Regicides who had listened unmoved to the King's words; not so Downes. "Have we hearts of stone?" he appealed to them, "Are we men?" Annoyed, they tried to quiet him, even to pull him down, for he showed signs of trying to get up to protest aloud. "If I die for it, I must do it," he gasped. At this Cromwell, who sat immediately in front of him, turned round: "What ails thee? Art thou mad? Canst thou not sit still and be quiet?" And Downes got out something like, "Sir,

no, I cannot be quiet," struggled to his feet, and in his loudest voice declared that he was not satisfied.

This whispering and fidgeting was intelligible to Bradshaw as a danger signal. There may have been other whispers and fidgeters among the weak, uneasy, frightened men. Certainly eleven years later Thomas Waite was to claim that he, too, had risen to protest; and others, too, would say that they had wanted the King's request to be granted.

Bradshaw, therefore, suddenly swerved away from his argument against further delay in the sentence, and concluded weakly that the Court would withdraw for consideration.

What happened in the next half hour we know only from the accounts given by some of the survivors in 1660. Downes, according to himself, stood up to Cromwell with all his puny strength and implored his colleagues to hear the King, who surely now was about to make offers in which they could settle the peace of the nation. Cromwell sneered and raged, called Charles "the hardest hearted man on earth" and Downes a peevish, troublesome fellow. At last Downes gave up in tears, and they went back to the Hall and left him. So, in his own defense, he told the tale eleven years later.

It seems probable that there was indeed a movement of genuine, anxious protest among the Commissioners and that some of them besides Downes vocally expressed their doubts. Cromwell—his nagging anxiety about Fairfax sharpened by the interruption in Court twenty minutes before—would have been in no mood to tolerate delay. He could easily have spoken of Charles in the way Downes later remembered; he certainly felt no trust at all in any offers he might make. He had experienced the King's advances, withdrawals, and evasions far too

often. His anger rallied his supporters and drove the waverers back into line.

When the King had been once again brought back to his chair, Bradshaw addressed him with renewed resolution, announcing that the Court would now proceed to the sentence.

Charles answered with a resigned irony: "Sir, I know it is in vain for me to dispute. I am no skeptic for to deny the power that you have; I know that you have power enough. . . ." Skirting lightly on the unlawfulness of their power, he went on to ask once again that he might be given opportunity to propound a new plan for the peace of the Kingdom to the Lords and Commons of his Parliament. Naturally it would cause a delay, "but a little delay of a day or two further may give peace, whereas an hasty judgment may bring on that trouble and perpetual inconveniency to the Kingdom, that the child that is unborn may repent it . . ."

It was thought by some at the time that what he intended to propose was his abdication in favor of his son. But no one was to know for certain because Bradshaw continued immovable in his rejection of the offer, although Charles made one last, vehement appeal: "If you will hear me, if you will give but this delay, I doubt not but I shall give some satisfaction to you all here, and to my people after that; and therefore I do require you (as you will answer it at the dreadful Day of Judgment), that you will consider it once again."

Bradshaw was unperturbed by the prospect of the Last Judgment; his conscience was clear. If the King had nothing more to say, he declared, the Court would proceed to sentence.

"Sir," said the King, "I have nothing more to say; but I shall desire that this may be entered, what I have said."

The moment had now come for Bradshaw's address to the prisoner, an oration which lasted about forty minutes. It was a creditable performance, garnished with a good deal of learning and presented with some dignity. He began by asserting the principal for which the war had been fought; that the King was subject to the law, and that the law proceeded from Parliament. Rather more uncertainly he added that it also proceeded from the people, and expounded on the significance of Parliament as the ultimate court of justice for the realm.

He went on to a rather farfetched comparison of Charles to Caligula and then proceeded to give examples of the manner in which kings, both in ancient and more recent times, had been accounted answerable for their crimes. As for the alleged hereditary right of the sovereign, Bradshaw had no difficulty in pointing out that this had frequently been passed over both in Scotland and in England. There were also precedents for calling kings to account: Edward II and Richard II had been deposed for their misdeeds, though these did not "come near to that height and capitalness of crimes that are laid to your charge."

He put it together deftly enough, but the task of legal and historical justification was a hopeless one. When he entered upon theory, he made a crucial point, and made it well: the authority of a ruler is valid only so long as he can offer protection in return. Here he touched the central core of government, and it was here that Charles had failed. Feudal society had been built on this principle: the overlord gave protection and the vassal paid with allegiance. English law and the English crown had grown from these beginnings. And it was a matter of practical experience that the ruler who failed in his primary task of protection could no longer expect to exact allegiance.

The King's friends might argue that the King had made war only in defense of his rights. But, rightly or wrongly, *he had made war on his subjects,* and in the crudest possible manner this violated the fundamental bond between him and his people.

Bradshaw went on to reiterate the charge: "Sir, the charge hath called you a Tyrant, a Traitor, a Murderer, and a Public Enemy to the Commonwealth of England. Sir, it had been well if that any of all these terms might rightly and justly have been spared, if any one of them at all."

The violence of the insult startled the King, who uttered an angry exclamation, unlike the contemptuous smile with which he had greeted these words a week before. They were indeed bitterly wounding to his dignity and his pride, since no more telling accusations could be made against a king.

The Lord President at some length explained why the words "Tyrant, Traitor, and Murderer" had to be used and went on to assert yet again the legal standing and the especial righteousness of the Court. He now, as one of the journalists reported, "pressed the King in a sweet manner to repent of his sins." He urged him to recognize his crimes and implore the forgiveness of God for bloodguiltiness. Unable to endure longer the stream of accusations, Charles interrupted.

"I would desire only one word before you give sentence; and that is, that you would hear me concerning those great imputations that you have laid to my charge."

It was far too late now for the King to answer the charge, and Bradshaw irritably told him so.

". . . You disavow us as a Court: and therefore for you to address yourself to us, not acknowledging us as a Court to judge of what you say, it is not to be permitted; and the truth is, all along, from the first time you were pleased to disavow and disown us, the Court needed not to have heard you one word . . ."

Overjustifying himself, determined now at all costs to stop the King from speaking again, he hurried on to the end, declared the King guilty, and commanded that the sentence be read. The Clerk read out the formula on which the Commissioners had agreed, briefly recapitulating the appointment of the Court, the charge, and the course of the trial, and concluded with the sentence: "that he the said Charles Stuart, as a Tyrant, Traitor, Murderer, and a public enemy, shall be put to death, by the severing of his head from his body."

At the conclusion of the reading the Commissioners rose to signify their agreement. The King, who had listened calmly to the last, now spoke. "Will you hear me a word, Sir?"

Bradshaw had not expected this request. A prisoner condemned to death was already dead in law and could not speak in Court. The fact was so familiar to him that it had not occurred to him that the prisoner did not know it. But the King, as he himself had said, was no ordinary prisoner. "You are not to be heard after the sentence," said Bradshaw, and ordered the guard to take him away.

The curt refusal dismayed the King. He had not believed that his trial would end with such abrupt brutality. He had been, all along, convinced that after the sentence he would be allowed to speak again. Now, suddenly, he saw that his last chance had gone, leaving him recorded and condemned as guilty simply by his silence. He could not believe the monstrous injustice.

"I may speak after the sentence—" he began; "by your favor, Sir, I may speak after the sentence ever." Then in growing agitation as the guards closed in, "By your favor, hold! The sentence, Sir—I say, Sir, I do—"

The guards were all round him ready to take him away by force. Then he found his voice for one last word: "I am not suffered for to speak: expect what justice other people will have."

As he went out, his servant John Joiner heard Colonel Axtell give his men the signal to cry out, so that he left the Hall to shouts of "Execution! Justice! Execution!" "Poor creatures," he said with a smile, "for sixpence they will say as much of their own commanders." The narrow corridors on the way back to Cotton House were thickly lined with the hostile troops, some of whom blew smoke in his face as he passed. Among them he saw an old palace servant, weeping. "You may forbid their attendance," said the King, "but not their tears."

Meanwhile the crowds dispersed from the Hall and the Commissioners went back into the Painted Chamber. John Downes, under what compulsion of curiosity or fear, had rejoined them. But their present business was short—merely to appoint some of their number to "consider of the time and place for the execution of the sentence against the King." After that they adjourned until Monday morning, having the intervening Sabbath for their thankful or anxious prayers.

The King, too, would be at prayer. He had no quiet and no privacy. The soldiers had been removed from his bedroom at the request of Herbert, the gentleman-in-attendance, who now slept there himself. As a guard he was certainly preferable to a couple of ordinary musketeers, and in these last unhappy days his behavior was not merely civil and correct. He seems to have shown, within the limits of his loyalty to the army, a genuine sympathy and human concern for the unfotunate King. For greater comfort, Charles had his chaplain. He had ordered his dogs to be removed. The greyhound Gypsy, the spaniel Rogue, his companions during all his imprisonment—these he found disturbing to his composure. His mind must now be turned to God alone. He did not know how long he had to prepare for death, but he knew his time would be short.

This article is taken from C. V. Wedgwood's new book, A Coffin for King Charles: The Trial and Execution of Charles I, *which will be published by Macmillan in August. Miss Wedgwood is a frequent contributor to* HORIZON. *Her last article, on Leo the Great and Attila the Hun, appeared in May, 1963.*

THE
EXECUTION
OF
CHARLES I

The King's death warrant required that he be put to death by the severing of his head from his body between the hours of ten in the morning and five in the afternoon on Tuesday, January 30. On the day before, he was allowed a farewell visit from two of his children—Princess Elizabeth, a plain, serious girl of thirteen, and Henry, Duke of Gloucester, a lively eight-year-old. (Of the King's children, only these two were in England. The three elder, Charles, Mary, and James, were in Holland, and the youngest, Henrietta, was with the Queen in Paris.) Charles spoke first to Elizabeth, who was crying bitterly. He had much of importance to say to her that he could say to no one else. He was anxious, not without cause, about adolescent jealousy between his two elder sons. She was to tell "her brother James, whenever she should see him, that it was his father's last desire, that he should no more look upon Charles as his eldest brother only, but be obedient unto him as his sovereign." The princess was crying so much that he could not be sure that she was taking it in. "Sweetheart, you will forget this," he said. She shook her head. "I shall never forget it whilst I live," and she promised to write it down. (It is thus from the account that she set down that night that we know what passed between them.) Then the King took little Henry on his knee. "Hark child, what I say," said he.

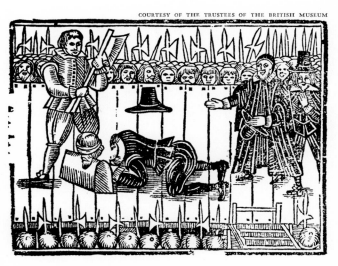

COURTESY OF THE TRUSTEES OF THE BRITISH MUSEUM

This woodcut, printed in 1649, is dramatic but inaccurate. The headsman actually wore a mask, a wig, and a thick false beard.

"They will cut off my head, and perhaps make thee a king; but you must not be a king so long as your brothers Charles and James do live; for they will cut off your brothers' heads (when they can catch them) and cut off thy head too, at last; and therefore I charge you, do not be made a king by them." With great firmness the child answered, "I will be torn in pieces first." This greatly pleased the King. He gave the children a few keepsakes, kissed and blessed them both, and sent them away.

Charles sat up reading and praying until nearly midnight, and then slept peacefully. At about six o'clock he drew back the bed curtain. "I will get up," he said, "having a great work to do this day." The bitter January frost was still unbroken, and he put on two shirts so that he would not shiver when he came to the block and so give an impression of fear. "I fear not death. Death is not terrible to me. I bless my God I am prepared." He spent an hour in prayer with Bishop Juxon and received the sacrament. At about ten o'clock, troops came for him, and, to the sound of beating drums, he was marched to Whitehall Palace. There followed a cruel three-hour delay while the House of Commons hurried through a bill making it illegal to proclaim a new king. Charles had intended that no food should pass his lips, on his last day, except the sacrament. The kindly, sensible Bishop persuaded him to eat a piece of bread and drink a glass of claret.

At last, at two o'clock, Charles was conducted along the palace corridors, between silent lines of soldiers standing shoulder to shoulder. The once beautiful palace had for some time been occupied by the army, and it was gloomy and bare. Charles walked through the Banqueting Hall (whose ceiling, painted for him by Rubens, represented the triumph of wisdom and justice over rebellion and falsehood), passed through one of the windows, and so came to the scaffold, which had been built against the palace wall. Here, before the Banqueting Hall, there was an open space, overlooked on three sides by the buildings of Whitehall. On the fourth side was a public street that ran right through the precincts of the palace, and across the street was the blank wall of the tiltyard. Obviously, this site had been chosen because it was a great deal more easily guarded than the usual places of public execution like Tower Hill or Tyburn. Large crowds had been waiting since early morning, but mounted troops formed a barrier between them and the scaffold, and Charles saw at once that it would be impossible to speak to them. Taking some notes from his pocket, he addressed himself instead to the group on the scaffold—soldiers, two colonels, several shorthand writers, the executioner and his assistant, and Bishop Juxon. Attesting his innocence, he asked God to forgive his enemies and care for the people. ("Truly I desire their liberty and freedom as much as anybody whomsoever; but I must tell you their liberty and freedom consists in having of government, those laws by which their life and their goods may be most their own. It is not for having a share in government, sir, that is nothing pertaining to them. A subject and a sovereign are clear different things. . . .") To the executioner, Charles explained that he would pray briefly and then sign for him to strike. Looking at the block, which was only ten inches from the ground, he asked if it could not be raised. The reason for the low block was to make the execution easier to perform if he had offered any resistance. "It can be no higher, sir," said the executioner, naturally unwilling to explain this. The King stood for a moment in prayer, and then lay down with his neck on the block. The executioner bent down to make sure that his hair was not in the way, and Charles, thinking that he was preparing to strike, said, "Stay for the sign." "I will, an' it please your Majesty," said the executioner.

A fearful silence had now fallen on the little knot of people on the scaffold, on the surrounding troops, and on the crowd. Within a few seconds the King stretched out his hands and the executioner on the instant and at one blow severed his head from his body.

A boy of seventeen, standing a long way off in the throng, saw the axe fall. He would remember as long as he lived the sound that broke from the crowd—"such a groan as I never heard before, and desire I may never hear again."

C.V.W.

THE DEPOT

A Terminal Case

Time ran out this year for Pennsylvania Station in New York. The high glass-and-steel-ceilinged train concourse, opposite, with its echoes of the Beaux-Arts and the age of train sheds, still stands as this is written, but outside the demolition men are taking away the classic colonnades and bringing down McKim, Mead & White's vaulted waiting room, a place huge enough to dwarf its original—the tepidarium of the Baths of Caracalla in Rome—and impress an earlier age with the power and majesty of the Pennsylvania Railroad. An even greater power, that which taxes and destroys, has levied $1,480,000 a year on this majestic landmark. And down it must come, to be replaced by glass-slab buildings of the modern era, including a new Madison Square Garden. What is happening here, said *The New York Times,* is "a monumental act of vandalism."

At the other extreme in size, the little Victorian Gothic depot on this page symbolizes tens of thousands of rural stations sharing a similar fate. It stands at Greycourt, once a suburban stop on the old Erie main line to western New York, and the ornamental roof and nonfunctional bell tower reflect the local pride which must have inspired its carpenter builder. The railroad station was an

important place in the great era of steam, a center of trade, politics, and dignified loafing. The automobile changed all that, and to a lesser extent, the airplane. Underpatronized and overtaxed, small-town stations (and some big-town ones) are simply crumbling away. A diminishing roster of passenger trains still go by Greycourt, but none has stopped there for years. By some fluke, the little building still stands—in company with a number of others which Mr. Plowden has recorded on the following pages.

From the very start of railroading—which came about in 1830 in both England and the United States—the construction of terminals, sheds, and waiting places along the line seemed to reflect a nearly religious awe of the smoking, steaming engine at the head end. You could scarcely stable this monster with the horses, or draw its carriages up to the inn as though it were the Royal Mail Coach or the Baltimore Stage. It had to have a special home of its own, and it was not long before this place began to resemble a temple. As early as 1839, a great Doric arch was set up as a grand entrance to Euston Station in

London, to remain a showplace for well over a century. Enormous stations quickly filled Europe, and a few decades later, in post-Civil War America, architects as notable as H. H. Richardson, Stanford White, and Louis Sullivan went to work for the prodigal railroad kings. No city or town was happy without its Greek, or Roman, or Gothic, or even Egyptian terminal. Domes and campaniles marked the great cities, towers and cupolas the small. At the very least, one could have something to keep the rain off the travelers in the style now called, less scornfully than in former days, "General Grant."

Everything passes. Railroad passenger travel is back to where it was about 1885, and caught in a dispiriting downward spiral. The station doors are locked and the passengers are back out in the rain. The steam engine went earlier, and with it much of the magic that lured men and boys to the depot. Uncle Sam may finally rescue the railroads (so far, to be sure, he only helps them in other countries), but nothing will save the old stations. Those who care for wildly eclectic architecture, and esteem the patina of neglect and decay, are commended to make their last inspections soon. The next visitors will be the archaeologists.   OLIVER JENSEN

The station at Jim Thorpe, Pennsylvania (which once went by the equally inelegant name of Mauch Chunk), is a splendid example of the spectacularly roofed "railroad style." It was a local showplace. Here summer visitors got out of Lehigh Valley Railroad trains for vacations in the surrounding Pocono Mountains. One can still get to Jim Thorpe on the Jersey Central, at another depot, but the Lehigh Valley, "Route of the Black Diamond," has stopped all its passenger service. The building will be torn down to make way for a supermarket.

DESERTED DEPOT: WILKES-BARRE, PA.

1887 STATION: EASTON, PA.

"GENERAL GRANT" ROOF: BETHLEHEM, PA.

ROMANESQUE REVIVAL: WHITE HOUSE, N.J.

When you mend windows instead of replacing them, it is clear the end is near. Since the picture opposite was taken, the last telegraph message has been sent from this office on the old Lehigh Valley; the station has been abandoned. The more substantial structures shown on this page still can be seen standing along the lines of the once-powerful Central Railroad of New Jersey. Jersey is hard on its railroads, and taxes them so heavily that this superb collection of Victoriana will before long be swept away.

ORIENTAL DOME, 1891: BAYONNE, N.J.

WINDOW REPAIRS: ROCHESTER JUNCTION, N.Y.

VICTORIAN SUBURBAN: NORTH BRANCH, N.J.

Considering the fact that only
four to six trains a day stop here
and that they will probably soon
be reduced to two, this is an
extraordinarily large station for
somnolent Canaan, Connecticut,
on the Danbury-Pittsfield line
of the bankrupt New Haven
Railroad. Once, however, this was
a busy junction, where the
New Haven met the Central
New England Railroad, on which
famous trains like the "Day
Express" ran from Boston to
Harrisburg, crossing the Hudson
River at Poughkeepsie. All that
remains of the famous Central in Connecticut today is the
wobbly Lakeville spur at the
right, whose eastern end is in
the woods behind the depot.

CANAAN

CARPENTER GOTHIC: TENAFLY, N.J.

There was money for elegance in the salad days of railroading. At the now-abandoned New Haven Railroad station at North Easton, H. H. Richardson, the line's famous architect, put lions' heads on his benches. Reading, with three converging lines and a hundred trains a day, got fancy doors; even little Tenafly, where Hetty Green took the cars, had cookie-cutter decorations. The sweep of platform and the size of the depot opposite suggest vast crowds—platoons of honeymooners, perhaps, boarding the Lehigh Valley main line, to the left, for Buffalo; brigades of businessmen on their way to New York or Toronto.

To the right, the single-track branch carried drummers and shoppers to Rochester. But all that is another generation and another country. Trains and passengers alike are gone now, and only the freights remain.

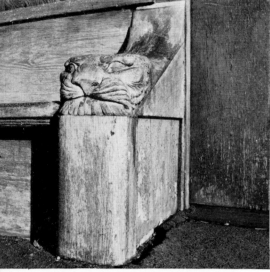

LION'S HEAD: NORTH EASTON, MASS.

SPIRAL STAIRS: WILKES-BARRE, PA.

IRON TIE-ROD SUNBURST: JERSEY CITY, N.J.

DEEP-CARVED DOORS: READING, PA.

ONLY GHOSTS BOOK TICKETS HERE

"ORNITHODELPHIA,
THE CITY OF BIRD LOVERS

PROJECT FOR THE PAVILION OF
CANINE PHRENOLOGY
AT THE WORLD'S FAIR·NEW YORK 1941

Mexico and Points East

Drawings by Pedro Friedeberg

Among the many marvels of the New York World's Fair, with its 641 acres of hallucinatory architecture—some of which seems impossible to imagine, let alone build—there is no pavilion by Pedro Friedeberg. More is the pity. He designed one (opposite, bottom), but for reasons that we have not gone into, it remains unbuilt. So do the rest of the buildings shown on these pages.

But who is Pedro Friedeberg? He himself has provided several answers to this question, so that one has a choice: "I was born in Italy during the era of Mussolini, who made all trains run on time. Immediately thereafter, I moved to Mexico where the trains are never on time, but where once they start moving they pass pyramids. My education was first entrusted to a Zapotec governess and later to such brilliant mentors as Mathias Goeritz, who taught me morals; José González, who taught me carpentry; and Gerry Morris, who taught me to play bridge. I have invented several styles of architecture, as well as one new religion and two salads. I am particularly fond of social problems and cloud formations. I am an idealist. I am certain that very soon now humanity will arrive at a marvelous epoch totally devoid of Knoll chairs or Danish coffee tables, and the obscenity of Japanese rock gardens five thousand miles from Kyoto." Or: "I am up at the crack of noon and after watering my geraniums, I breakfast off things Corinthian. Later in the day I partake of an Ionic lunch followed by a Doric nap. On Tuesdays I sketch a volute or two, and perhaps a pediment, if the mood overtakes me. Wednesday I have set aside for washing socks. On Thursdays I usually relax, whereas on Friday I write autobiographies."

Although Friedeberg's autobiographies tend, like his breakfasts, to be Corinthian, there are some plain Doric facts in them. He was indeed born in Italy (in 1937), was brought to Mexico at a very early age, studied architecture at the Ibero-American University in Mexico City, and later became a pupil of the German-Mexican painter and sculptor Mathias Goeritz. He has had one-man shows of his drawings in Mexico City, New York, Paris, Lisbon, and Munich. He also designs chairs and clocks. The chairs, shown at left, are handmade of Mexican mahogany and sell for about 350 dollars. Buy one, and Pedro Friedeberg will have you in the palm of his hand.

OPPOSITE: *The buildings in Friedeberg's* Ornithodelphia *have been helpfully identified by the artist as, from left to right, a psychiatric ward for retired hummingbirds, the Reformed Church of St. Audubon, a bank with murals by Paolo Uccello ("bird" in Italian), and the Nightingale Night Club. The Pavilion of Canine Phrenology is unfortunately absent from Flushing Meadows. Didn't the Fair officials get the design in time? Or were they afraid of going to the dogs?*

OVERLEAF: *Of the* Motel Halfway between Xochimilco and Fontainebleau *there is much to say, and Friedeberg has said it: "On the northwest we see the Wing for Incognito Travelers flanked by the Court of Good Manners and the Court of Bad Manners. In the center is a mental telepathy station and the School for Hairsplitting. In the foreground is the restaurant—famous for the Oxtail Soup Boycotts of 1948. Cavorting on the distant roofs are waitresses in full uniform."*

55

At the left is Madame Pompadour's Radar Machine *with which,* "*at an inclination of fifteen degrees and aided by Rameau's nephew, she managed to intercept Frederick the Great's bombers." Below are* The Individual Bungalows for Nuns near Phoenix, Arizona *with "the famous shadows cast by the five o'clock sun." The drawing opposite is called* The Origin of Marmalade (II). *According to Friedeberg, it is "A stunning jam factory alternating between the Tactless and Vitruvian styles. The orange tree on the sixth floor is really a tangerine tree. The hands near the penthouses warn stray airplanes to keep off. The sky is in the Ominous style."*

THREE WEEKS

After fourteen years of Communism, China — whatever else it may be —

Statues of Mao, a nude, and doves of peace grace a shop window in Peking. Loudspeakers blare out "Chairman Mao Is Always With Me."

China begins—if one is flying by the quickest route from the West—at Irkutsk, where one changes planes. The Siberian mountains, with their dense pine forests and their patches of year-round snow, merge into the arid hills that surround the Mongolian desert. It is as spectacular a journey as any on earth, and it emphatically achieves the effect from which air, travel derives what interest it may have: that of a dramatic transfer from one climate and one civilization to another.

Much of my attention, however, remained inside the plane. It was a Soviet Ilyushin, but it belonged to Chinese Airways, and thus I was effectively in China for the first time in my life. The hostesses, living up to expectations, wore blue jackets and trousers. They were small and trim, affording (to my taste) a welcome change from the amply proportioned blondes who embody the Russian ideal of feminine charm. The impression they conveyed, one of combined delicacy and sturdiness, was to become familiar as the hallmark of everything Chinese from a bridge to a table and from a woman to a teapot.

After about ten minutes, one of the hostesses inquired if I would like something to read. I accepted, and she handed me a pamphlet entitled "More on the Differences between Comrade Togliatti and Ourselves." It was in Esperanto. In the ensuing three weeks such pamphlets were to become a well-recognized aspect of the Chinese scene. They appeared in hotel lounges, in

office waiting rooms, in railroad dining cars. They were available in English and in Vietnamese, in Spanish and in Thai.

My presence thirty thousand feet above the Gobi desert was something that I owed to the peculiarities of Chinese visa policy. Western journalists rank high on the list of foreign devils. There are in fact no correspondents of non-Communist newspapers in Peking (there are two agency men, one from Reuters and the other from Agence France Presse). The *Observer*, a British Sunday paper to which I contribute, had repeatedly tried to get a man into China; but even its drama critic, who quite genuinely wanted to write about the Chinese theatre, was refused a visa.

At this point, someone discovered that a small travel agency ran three-week tours to China twice a year. The *Observer* asked me to sign on. I did so, without any great hopes of ever getting as far as London Airport. It is true that "novelist" appears on my passport in the space that says "profession," and it is also true that I am a novelist; but I have written too many newspaper and magazine articles to be able to claim that novel-writing is my sole occupation, and it seemed prudent to expect the Chinese scrutineers of visa applications to discover this. But I exaggerated either their vigilance or my reputation. The visa came through.

Later, when my prudence had been melted by amiability and rice wine, I told the guides who accompanied the tour that I was going to write articles about my visit. They were delighted. Nor did they alert the authorities; when I left China, my notes and camera film passed the customs without attracting a glance. The explanation is that in Communist countries a deep gulf divides the writer from the journalist. The former is an esteemed intellectual, the latter a despicable hireling of imperialism.

"Conducted tour" is such a dirty word that I need hardly caution readers against expecting to find here an account of typical conditions in China—if that could mean much, anyway, in so huge and so rapidly changing a country. I always took it for granted that the school, factory, or housing development we were being shown was on the approved list for foreign visitors, and by that token was not typical. So much was evident to the eye. Returning from a visit to a commune, one had only to look at houses or at people's clothes to know when the bus had left it and was passing another commune *not* on the tourist circuit.

Still, it is fair to give our guides credit on two counts. They made no attempt to hide these disparities. They would, in fact, call our attention to a huddle of slums—and Chinese slums, decidedly, are slums—to comment: "You see what a task we have

IN THE MIDDLE KINGDOM

is still Chinese

By MERVYN JONES

ahead of us." Also, if any of us chose to skip an item on the itinerary, we were free to wander about as we pleased and to talk to such people as we could find who spoke English, these being reasonably numerous in places like Canton and Shanghai.

My lengthiest conversations, however, were with the guides themselves (there were fresh ones in each of the six cities we went to, in addition to the two who traveled with us). The guides were, it goes without saying, "politically reliable." They were almost all young, and their minds had been formed under the Communist regime. It was fascinating to see how these minds worked.

A discussion with a Chinese—and maybe this has nothing much to do with Communism—is always in the nature of an intellectual contest. This is especially the case when he does not wish to answer a question. Never will he do anything so crude as to turn surly or to invent a lie. No: he will reply with a phrase that appears informative, its ingenuity residing in the fact that it actually contains no information. The favorite in my collection came when I asked how often there is a flight from Moscow to Peking. "There is a daily plane," I was smilingly informed, "but not necessarily every day."

I met a similar *fin de non-recevoir*, to employ the useful diplomatic phrase, when I asked a young man what happened in China when an unmarried woman has a child. He gave the routine reply that this, though common in the bad old days of the Kuomintang, now seldom occurred. Doubtless, I said; but if it did? He rubbed his chin dubiously and asked what would happen in England. I answered that the parents might marry; if not, the baby was usually adopted. After a pause, he said: "Approximately the same is the position in China."

On another occasion, I asked whether there is rationing in China. The answer was: "We have planned distribution, to ensure that all receive enough."

"But how much meat, for instance, can each person buy?"

"As much as he needs. That is the purpose of the system."

"He can't buy as much as he wants, then?"

"It would be absurd to want more meat than one needs."

I have summarized this exchange, which lasted fully half an hour. At the end of this time I was hoarse and exasperated, and no doubt presented an unpleasant picture of the boorish Westerner. The Chinese, bland and imperturbable, had still not conceded that rationing was in force. At last he said with a sympathetic air: "I am afraid that, since you live in an unjust society, it is difficult for you to understand our system."

"There is probably no kitsch like Chinese kitsch." At Peking's Institute of Fine Arts pupils sculpture heroic figures for public monuments.

These examples indicate that the young Chinese, in striking contrast to the young Russian nowadays, does not imagine that he can learn anything from the West. To judge by those I met, their ignorance of life beyond their own borders is stunning, although perhaps no greater than that of Russians before the death of Stalin. This ignorance is exceeded only by their lack of interest. In my three weeks in China, only one person asked me anything about my own country or about any other country that I had visited. He was a university graduate, and his question was: "Is it still possible to buy and sell Negroes in the United States?"

From the Chinese point of view, they do not need to learn anything because they already know. One gentleman, this time a middle-aged official, treated me to a detailed description of conditions in Yugoslavia. The interesting thing about this little lecture was not that everything he said was untrue: that was to be expected. What was remarkable was that it had been made clear beforehand that I had been to Yugoslavia and that he had not. This did not, in his eyes, give me any advantage, but merely made it more necessary for him to dispel the misconceptions instilled in me by the Tito clique of revisionists.

It would be an error to think, as Western liberals sometimes do, that the Chinese are smarting under their exclusion from international society. If the Peking government were given a seat in the United Nations, it would no doubt send its representatives

59

for the sake of whatever advantages were to be gained, but without any particular sense of gratification. The Chinese Communists, of course, regard the U.N. much as Lenin regarded the League of Nations. The fact that the United States does not recognize the effective government of China is not spoken of by the Chinese as an insult but simply as the biggest joke since the explorer looked at the giraffe and said, "I don't believe it."

In all this, Communism has done no more than to reinforce traditional Chinese attitudes. One of the names the Chinese have for their own country is Chung-kuo. Western writers usually translate this as "the Middle Kingdom," but that gives only a pale idea of its significance. The Chinese think of their civilization as central in their view of the world, as something within

PHOTOS FERNAND GIGON

Both the Latin alphabet and Chinese characters are taught in Chinese schools, "but anyone . . . really educated will use Chinese characters."

which they are born and into which others may perhaps aspire to enter. Their invariable courtesy restrains them from putting this assumption into words. But, unless he is quite insensitive, the traveler—whether English, American, or Russian—cannot be unaware that he is regarded as a recently educated barbarian from the outer fringe.

This is not to say, however, that China excludes either the science or the culture of the outside world. What one finds, in every field, is an evenhanded dualism. That which is not Chinese is dubbed "international" and enjoys an equal prestige—no more, and no less. There is "international" athletics, and there is Chinese athletics. There is Swedish drill, and the graceful Wu Su system of slow-motion exercises; to watch scores of people performing them in the park on their way to work, or on a platform while waiting for a train, is to feel that one has chanced upon an undress rehearsal for a historical movie. There is "international" chess, and there is Chinese chess—as well as an even more complicated game called "surrounding chess," in which you hem in but never take your opponent's pieces.

Hospitals, too, have "international" and Chinese departments. The primary technique of Chinese medicine is acupuncture. This business of sticking needles into patients is considered mere quackery by some Western doctors, but others have been seriously impressed by it. Its theory cannot be justified in ortho-

dox physiological terms—but, after all, the same can be said of psychoanalysis. Be that as it may, I had expected to find rival parties in the medical world—traditionalists extolling acupuncture, the modern-minded, and presumably the Communists, rejecting it. But this is not how things happen in China.

A student takes a six-year course to qualify in "international" medicine. If he wishes, he can then study for another four years and take a degree in Chinese medicine. Some older doctors are qualified only in the latter. A hospital has both on its staff, and the patient may choose by which method he will be treated.

The two disciplines are on terms not merely of co-existence but of co-operation. In difficult cases "international" and Chinese specialists confer. I was myself suffering, as the aftermath of a broken leg, from an obstinate swelling around the ankle which had not yielded to physiotherapy back in England. I asked an acupuncturist if he could do anything about it. He said yes, but only by working in conjunction with "international" methods.

I then asked him what ailments were best treated by acupuncture. In the first place, he replied, depression, insomnia, and anxiety states; secondly, rheumatoid conditions; thirdly, asthma and bronchial troubles. All these were related, in his view, for the concept of psychosomatic disease and of the unity of mind and body has been accepted by Chinese medicine for centuries.

In the arts, too, there are parallel tracks. In one room of a Palace of Culture—or, as we should more prosaically call it, an evening college*—one will find an amateur orchestra rehearsing Brahms. Down the corridor, another group will be rendering Chinese compositions on such instruments as the Mongolian lute and the two-stringed violin.

*T*he Chinese opera retains its traditional forms, which have scarcely altered since the fifteenth century. These forms are artificial and symbolic to a degree unmatched anywhere on earth. To follow the action of a Chinese opera requires the mastery of a series of codes: codes of dress which indicate status, codes of make-up which indicate character, codes of gesture which indicate emotion. Realism is eschewed; an audience would be insulted if an actress were actually to weep instead of making the "weeping" gesture. To grow up in China, of course, is to understand these conventions as an American understands football tactics or a Spaniard the nuances of bullfighting. The Chinese opera is in no sense a minority art. In Hankow, a city of about one million people, I went to the People's Paradise, a complex of theatres ranged around a vast courtyard. There are fourteen stages, and the total seating capacity is thirty-three thousand.

But the theatres work on the repertory system; the stage on which a traditional opera is presented on Monday will be occupied by a modern play on Tuesday. I went to one on my own, and found realistic sets, everyday costumes, lighting, and dialogue spoken in natural voices—all just like a play in the West, but all of which are absent from the traditional spectacle. The play was about the Japanese occupation, and resembled any wartime Hollywood movie about the Resistance and the Gestapo. I had no difficulty in following the story without knowing Chinese, from which I conclude that it was somewhat lacking in subtlety.

The most curious situation relates to writing. The Chinese system of characters has the advantage that what is written can

*Or, in the unromantic United States, night school.

be read regardless of pronunciation, in the same way as figures. As I appreciated in Canton, where the guides who had come with us from the north could not make themselves understood by local people, this is not something to be lightly discarded. Nevertheless, the characters are a barrier to mass literacy. (This remains true even though they have recently been simplified in form and —for the older generation—robbed of much of their beauty.)

Accordingly, there is an increasing use of the Latin alphabet. Street signs, shop names, and public notices appear both in characters and (as the Chinese say) in spelling. As a matter of fact, the spelling of well-known names looks distinctly unfamiliar to the Western visitor, but this is not the fault of the Chinese. The transliteration of characters adopted in the nineteenth century was quite inaccurate phonetically, and the Chinese have replaced it. Peking thus becomes Beijing, which is how it is pronounced.

At various times since the Communists took power, it has been reported that China has switched over to Latinization, has halted the change, or has resumed it. Here again, this is not how things happen. The intention is to have *both* the Latin alphabet and Chinese characters. Spelling will be used as a quick method of teaching illiterates, and also children, to read. People who have mastered only the alphabet will be able to understand signs written in it, but anyone with a claim to consider himself really educated will use Chinese characters.

Of the several paradoxes displayed by contemporary China, the most obvious is that between an ancient civilization and a modern political dogma. My impression is that this has presented no particular problem to the Communists. Like all successful revolutionaries, they have made their revolution appear as a renewal. The visible symbol of this is the lavish restoration of the beauties of the past. One of the showpieces of the Summer Palace, just outside Peking, is the Long Corridor. Its walls and beams are decorated with ten thousand pictures, either landscapes or historical and legendary scenes. All of them have lately been repainted; and this is only one case of an obviously well-calculated policy.

It is in this context that one has to consider the position of Mao Tse-tung. At first sight the matter seems simple enough, and disagreeable enough, too. Slogans exhort the populace to "march forward under the banner of Chairman Mao." Children write essays about his life; bookstores display his collected speeches on special tables; his portrait adorns homes and classrooms, offices and teahouses. The insistently plugged tune of "Chairman Mao Is Always With Me" streams over the loudspeakers. The visitor feels that he knows quite well what all this is about—especially when he observes the not infrequent pictures of Stalin, ranked with Marx, Engels, Lenin, and Mao as a saint of the official religion. (You can even buy silk table mats with these five faces.)

But this is China. In the Imperial Palace in Peking, there is a wall lined with stone tablets. Each is a poem written by one of the emperors and copied by a stonecutter in the emperor's handwriting. Calligraphy, like poetry, is an art form of importance.

In various public places, we saw inscriptions written vertically. Vertical writing is still used for poetry, though horizontal writing is now normal for most purposes. We were always told that this was a poem by Mao; and the guide never failed to add that his calligraphy had been faithfully reproduced. These poems kept turning up—carved in cedarwood, incised in marble walls, em-

broidered on silk, engraved on ivory. One sees more poems by Mao, indeed, than portraits of him. In book form they are even more often on sale than his speeches and political writings. I read through a translation. The poems are lyrical, often devoted to the beauties of nature, and seldom concerned with Communist ideology. In point of fact, Mao is regarded by non-Communist scholars as a highly talented poet in the mainstream of Chinese tradition. But he does not write poetry, as Churchill paints, for mere relaxation: both the writing and the organized publicity given to it serve a purpose. They establish that Mao, as much as any emperor in the golden ages of the past, is a man of culture. He knows that this matters.

Confronted from my first day in Peking with what I have called

While some women work at communes, such as the one above in Peking, "many . . . do not work, or work at more domestic occupations."

the most obvious of Chinese paradoxes, I became aware, as I traveled, of another which has not received much comment. Officially, China is under the sway of the most doctrinaire and fanatical form of Communism, unadulterated by the compromises to which Russia has yielded. Whether this is regarded as worthy of praise, condemnation, or alarm, it is seldom questioned. But in reality Mao's regime has watered down Marxist principles in a variety of respects. I shall give three instances.

Religious belief, except of course for Party members, is a private matter. I should not care to assert, without an investigation that a tourist patently cannot conduct, that there is real religious freedom in China. I will only mention that I saw well-attended services in Buddhist temples, and that the authorities seemed to be remarkably accommodating toward them. May Day last year coincided with a major holy day for Buddhists (the latter being a movable occasion, like our Easter). It was arranged that the official celebrations should be over by noon, leaving the afternoon free for Buddhist worship; since I was in Peking at the time, I was able to verify this. What most surprised me, however, was to be told that the Communist Party conducts no anti-religious propaganda. There is no Chinese equivalent to the League of Militant Atheists, which still exists and is intermittently reactivated in Russia. When I described its functions, the Chinese Communists listened with amusement. Of course, they may have been pulling the wool over my eyes, but since I described myself as a non-believer and professed to be shocked by their dereliction of duty, I think it unlikely.

Then, there are people in China living on profits from private business. A certain, though diminishing, number of small shops, restaurants, and craft workshops are still privately owned. A great many more—including quite large undertakings—are, to cite the official explanation, jointly operated. I was soon familiar with the sign *gong si* over a store front or a factory entrance. It means "State and private." The prerevolutionary owner, unless he was active in politics on the Kuomintang side, is receiving out of current profits a guaranteed annual sum equal to 5 per cent of the capital value of the business. He may also be the manager,

Old and new co-exist in China today, but there is little evidence of the new in this Peking square with its ancient Heavenly Peace Gate.

drawing a salary as well as his 5 per cent, but he may be doing no work at all. True enough, the State has all the power in this supposed partnership. The fact remains that the capitalist is sometimes getting money for nothing, in defiance of Marx's pledge that "the expropriators will be expropriated" and of the dogma "to each according to his work."

In Hangchow there is a pleasant park, about fourteen acres in extent, which was formerly a private garden. I asked what had been done with the house, built as a week-end retreat by a prominent Shanghai capitalist. The surprised reply was that this gentleman, though he had sold the garden to the municipality, still owned the house. A fence, indeed, excluded the public as positively as in Sussex or Connecticut. Had he not, however, a house in Shanghai? Yes, certainly he had. I remarked that in Czechoslovakia, as a measure of social justice and to meet the housing shortage, there is a law forbidding anyone to own more than one residence. This seemed to the Chinese an intolerant restriction.

Again, in the outskirts of Shanghai I noticed a gang of workmen building what was obviously a fair-sized private house. The guide assured me that it was legitimate to have a house built for oneself. But what sort of people, I asked, could afford it? He replied blandly, "capitalists, mostly."

What most confounded my expectations in China, however, was to see very little sign of that ruthless emphasis on basic pro-

duction, at the expense of everyday consumer needs, which is the hallmark of what the Russians (and the Chinese) call "socialist construction." The first five-year plan in Russia was the time when whole new industries were equipped, when vast dams and power projects were put in hand, and when the output of coal and steel went up four times over. It was also the time when people worked till they dropped, when there were food queues in the cities and famines in the country and you could not buy a shoe-lace or a saucer. One expects the "great leap forward"—according to the Chinese, still in progress—to be like that. It is not.

The Chinese Communists have been in power for fourteen years. Three members of our tourist party had visited Russia in 1931, fourteen years after the Revolution. They agreed that the progress made by China in the same time span was greater.

A dictatorial regime can conceal a great many blemishes, especially for the short-stay tourist. For instance, it can round up all the beggars, as Mussolini did. But it cannot hide the kind of crude and elemental poverty that confronts the traveler in India, say, as soon as he steps out of his hotel. The thing is too big to control. Compared with Europeans, and still more with Americans, the millions in China are very poor, and doubtless will be so for decades. A comparison with India (where I have been) is more relevant, and I shall record it in terms of a scene that cannot have been staged. On my first morning in Hankow, I went out alone for a walk before breakfast. A white face in a Chinese street, especially in an inland city, causes a sensation, and soon I was surrounded by about a hundred staring children. Not one was in rags; not one had running eyes, or sores on his face; not one looked skinny or underfed.

There may have been hunger in the critical years of 1959 and 1960, and there may be hunger now in remote places away from the main railroad lines. But I saw no hunger in days of walking round the towns and days more of travel by slow train the length of China. The rice ration—I finally got the figures, and checked them elsewhere—is twenty kilos, or forty-four pounds, a month. The meat ration is normally one or one and a half pounds a month; most Chinese have a vegetable diet. Chickens, fish, and eggs are unrationed and always seemed to be plentiful. Prices are high in terms of wages, but not impossibly so. On a railroad platform, you could buy a whole roast duck for two yuan—$1.25 on the exchange rate, and about half a day's wage. I never saw a queue for food, other than a dozen people waiting to be served at the numerous little stalls that sell cakes and snacks.

Nor was I ever conscious—and on this point, to be sure, one can report only the most superficial impression—of an intensity of effort. Whether at communes or in factories, workers made leisurely pauses to stare at the foreign visitors. At one commune, which was a tea plantation, nobody was working at all, except five girls who were picking tea by themselves in an otherwise deserted expanse. Mr. Lo, the "brigade leader," explained that it was a holiday. The girls had volunteered to pick tea for half an hour so that the tourists could photograph them.

We asked why it was a holiday. Because of the rain, said Mr. Lo. Triumphantly seeing through this piece of Communist duplicity, we pointed out that it was not raining. Mr. Lo replied that it had been raining when he got up, he had ordered a day off, and now it was too late to change his mind.

All this may have been an elaborate swindle. Yet, to say the least, production is hardly being pursued at all costs if a day's labor can be sacrificed for the sake of convincing British tourists to revise their notions of commune life.

In China, as in other Communist countries, women work in the fields, in steel plants, on construction sites, and at other jobs that would be handled only by men in the West. A good many women, however, do not work, or work at more domestic occupations. In a village one may see them on their doorsteps weaving baskets or spinning, as well as strolling about, shopping, and looking after their children. A road-repair gang, for example, will be 80 per cent male in China; it is the other way about in Russia. At a large commune near Canton I got some figures that bore out this impression. There were eleven thousand families, and the labor force totaled eighteen thousand. Since boys mostly leave school at thirteen, and many families would thus provide more than one male worker, it is evident that a fair proportion of women do not form part of the labor force.

This is neither so curious nor so virtuously humanitarian as it may appear. Traveling in China, one comes to think in a new way of the enormous and constantly increasing population. It is indeed true that population pressure constitutes a problem, especially as there are so many children below working age. This is why the Communists, although they pretend to visitors that there is no such problem and declare that the forebodings of Malthus are "a reactionary philosophy," are conducting a vigorous birth-control campaign. But there is another side to the coin. These innumerable mouths—or at all events most of them—are also hands. While Soviet Russia has always had to contend with an acute labor shortage, China has labor enough and to spare.

Therefore, a surprising number of people are busied in making paper lanterns, silk flags, jade and ivory statuettes, sandalwood boxes, and teapots decorated with faint cloud-capped mountains. Some of these things are exquisite and some are banal in the extreme, for there is probably no kitsch like Chinese kitsch. But they exist in ample quantities, and so do manufactured goods like watches, ballpoint pens, microscopes, and vacuum cleaners, which in many instances were not made in China until about ten years ago. If one were to walk out of the People's Central Department Store in Peking and travel westward across the Communist world, one would reach Prague before finding another store so well filled with consumer goods.

*T*he pleasure of traveling in China—and in this matter I do not imagine that Communism has made much difference one way or the other—is that one constantly rediscovers the natural good taste and love of beauty that are, if not universal, at least widespread and well esteemed. At one hotel I admired the plates and cups. They were of a luminous light-blue, on which a white flying crane was embossed in relief. Could I find a shop, I asked, where they were on sale? Apparently not; they were specially made for this hotel and had been designed by the manager. I then inquired whether this manager had formerly worked in the ceramic industry. No, he had not. It was merely that he liked things to look well. He had designed the dining-room chairs and the curtains, too.

It is perfectly true that in China, as in most other parts of the world, many of the things in the shops are financially beyond the reach of the ordinary family. But, against a background of absolute poverty, a little goes a long way. At the tea-growing commune, I was taken into a village home. The midday meal, of rice and vegetables in a set of pleasing little bowls, was on the table. The eldest son took me to see his room. He was about to get married, and he had bought a double bed, a chest, and a closet— somewhat rashly, perhaps, since these objects so filled the room that one could hardly turn around. Being an amateur musician, he owned a Chinese lute and a Western-style violin. He also had a clock and a radio. When he was a child, he said, he had slept on the floor and the whole family had eaten from a common bowl.

I am far from citing even this modest degree of affluence as typical. This man was a "team leader" at an exceptionally pros-

Old and new again: modern buildings line the shore, while a ferry-boat is poled across one of the many lakes that dot Peking's parks.

perous commune, singled out to receive the visits of foreigners. It is certain that plenty of Chinese families still sleep on the floor and own practically nothing. The direction of movement, however, is what matters.

In these necessarily scattered observations, I have singled out certain themes: the durability of Chinese civilization; the intricate and formalized expressions that it has found, of which the opera is only one; and the dualism that permits the "international" and the Chinese to exist side by side. It may be objected that I have said little about China under Communism. But, if we have learned anything from closer acquaintanceship with Communism in Russia, it is that a political system can redirect but cannot remodel the material which it inherits. The Soviet Communists were imagined, by their detractors, to have wiped out all accepted values and pressed the population into a rigid mold; by their worshipers, to have banished greed and cruelty and instilled a new and higher morality. When the dust cleared, Russians were discerned still beating their wives and drinking too much vodka—and still sleeping in corners to make room for unexpected second cousins.

Approximately the same, as my young acquaintance would have said, is the position in China.

The British writer Mervyn Jones is the author of The Antagonists, *from which an excerpt appeared in the July, 1962,* HORIZON.

ALWAYS
BE THANKFUL
WHEN YOU
CATCH WHALES

By STAN STEINER

North of the Arctic Circle, on the icy fingers of land that border on the Chukchi Sea, there is the tiny Eskimo village of Point Hope. By the most recent nose count the Eskimos of this Alaskan settlement, some three hundred and twenty-four inhabitants, own twenty-five "magic machines"—their name for the Japanese tape recorders that have captivated the igloo market.

One tape recorder for every thirteen Eskimos!

Hunters of the polar bear celebrate a kill. But before the banquet of bear meat they tell the tale of their heroism, how they stalked the Goliath and how they killed him, to the spinning magnetic tapes. . . . It is a new moon and the "Song of Allingnuk," the Giver of Whales, is sung by the wives of the whaling-boat captains. Go bring out the tape recorders. . . . Young lovers are to be joined in Eskimo marriage. Record the wedding ceremony. . . . Sealing time has come and the little seals, the *nachik*, are stripped of their skins and cleaned and dried. Record the work songs. . . . Caribou has been hunted and the aromatic "ice cream" of the Arctic, the *akootuk*, is to be boiled from the suet of the animal. Then seal oil must be added, and the frothy, snow-white soufflé frozen; it is much the same as frozen custard. Record the recipe. . . . *Oogruk*, the huge bearded seals, have been sighted near the village. Umiaks, the open whaleboats, set sail in the narrow ice channels, in pursuit. The old men sing to the success of the hunt. Record these songs too. . . .

On the icebound coast and in the inland settlements that burrow under a labyrinth of snow, the recorders wind and unwind the long hours of the Arctic night. Eskimos gather in sod igloo and log hut, not merely for social contact, but to record their vanishing culture before the jukeboxes of the youngsters drown it out with the wail of the Twist, "that animal dance," as the elders call it.

All this is a kind of reverse of the usual situation, where the professors and researchers descend with their equipment on some remote culture—which usually doesn't care whether it is recorded for history or not. But the Eskimos are creating a do-it-yourself anthropology, and the johnny-come-lately researchers of the future may find themselves quite useless. From Kwigillingok to Koyuk, Klu-

kwan to Kwethluk, Kotzebue to Kalskag, Eek to Goodnews Bay—there are few villages not adept at modulating the treble or lowering the bass. And it would appear that there are few family circles that do not own their own "magic machines," for their personal pleasure and for the edification of visiting anthropologists.

Because of their geographical isolation, the Eskimos have been one of the most reticent of all the native people on the continent. Turn-of-the-century traders and explorers found them remarkably hard to tempt with the lures of a mechanized civilization. Even today, such developments as the supermarket and the automobile have a negligible influence on the frugal lives of the Eskimos, who still cling to subsistence hunting as a way of life. The reluctant acceptance by them of "non-native" culture, where it has occurred, has been largely due to practical necessity: an outboard motor for a whaling boat, a store-bought steel knife, a cooking stove for blubber.

Weather no doubt has played a major part in helping the Eskimos to avoid the usual fate of so many indigenous peoples of the Americas. Temperatures of 60 below zero have undoubtedly cooled the enthusiasm of many entrepreneurs, but the native character is obdurate, too. Until the tumultuous arrival of the present teen-age generation, the Eskimos have kept their traditions deep-frozen and almost untouched.

The Tundra Times, a newspaper of the Eskimos, Aleuts, and Indians of Alaska, has commented on this ironically: "In the case of the Arctic people, it is a well-known fact that they do not feel that civilization is adverse altogether. They have accepted many of the fine things civilization has to offer. On the other hand, the Eskimos especially, are resisting those things that seek to undermine their culture."

How, then, have the tape recorders charmed the reluctant Eskimos?

Although Eskimos have a written language, it is not generally known to Alaskan Eskimos and hence, until these handy devices arrived, there was no recorded literature. English, their language of literacy, is the speech of the children, learned in government schools. The old people, the traditional leaders of community life, use English mainly out of politeness to strangers—and when they have to talk to the tax collector. In their daily lives the Eskimo tongue prevails.

Legends of the past, ceremonials, and the songs of celebration and religion have had to be memorized. Much of this ancient lore has been lost in the endless retelling, from generation to generation. But magnetic tape has made it possible to halt this atrophy of a culture and thus preserve the best legends as passed on by the best "teller" in the village.

The "Song of Allingnuk," transcribed in this fashion, tells of Nikuwanna, the young wife of a whaling captain who on the spring night of a new moon, dons a beautiful squirrel-skin parka, climbs out of the *pallisuk*, the sky hole of her igloo, and lifts a stone vessel in prayer to the "Dweller of the Moon." She sings:

O, Allingnuk, Dweller of the Moon,
Allingnuk, great and generous Giver of Whales,
I, Nikuwanna, whose wife I am of Killigvuk,
A young and hopeful new whaler of Tigara,
Implore thee for thy life-giving gift.

One of the venerable Eskimo singers, Jimmy Killigvuk, who at seventy-one professes to remember the coming of the first white man to Point Hope (the Tigara of the song), has recorded a number of the old songs. Here is his mocking version of the "Eskimo Woman's Love Song," with its understated envoy:

Here I am sitting
  And I am sitting still.
And I see two kayaks coming.
  Here I am sitting
And I am sitting still.
  And two men are coming
  To court me.
And here I am a ne'er-do-well
And not very good-looking.

Killigvuk has also recorded a hunting song which came down from his great-great-great-grandfather Karairnok:

Who am I?
  Watch me! I am at the mouth of the river!
I have killed the caribou and the oogruk!
  I have also killed the whale!
Who am I?
  Watch me! I am at the mouth of the river!
I sing a song to Sunikpeak.
  Sunikpeak did not get a caribou.
He did not get an oogruk.
  He did not get a whale.
The reason Sunikpeak did not get these animals:
  Because he has a long, long beard.

Songs of this sort, enlivened by the mock-heroic boast and the rejoinder so typical of the Eskimo's sardonic humor, have a buoyancy that probably would be dulled by the techniques of scholarly field workers. In doing their own tape recording the Eskimos seem to feel free to be themselves. In similarly intimate surroundings they record their dances, while an announcer identifies the persons who are dancing and describes their gestures.

"Letters" preserved on tape recorders journey from village to village. These have become the spoken newspapers of the North. Once the teller of a letter has recorded his message on his magic machine, he sends it, by umiak or dog sled, to his relatives far down the coast, or to a lonely inland settlement where it is welcomed much as a nomad troubadour of old. It has the advantage that nothing has been lost in translation.

These Eskimo letters are often orchestrated by a whole community, which gives them a choral effect. In the neighboring villages a communal communication of this sort is eagerly awaited. Local government matters and meetings of officials are recorded in a similar way. When the Inupiat Paitot ("People's Heritage") Conference was convened in Kotzebue last year, the speeches and discussions were taped and sent home with the delegates to their constituents. And it was suggested that such a procedure might have a salutary effect if it were instituted elsewhere. When officials of the Atomic Energy Commission came to Point Hope to hear the objections of the Eskimo leaders to the proposed "Project Chariot"—the explosion of a nuclear device in the area of Cape Thompson to create a polar harbor (a plan since shelved)—the proceedings were recorded by *two* tape recorders, kept "going full blast."

The most unusual and perhaps most important use of the magic machines by the Eskimos has been in the preservation of their folkways. It has helped to unify the scattered people of the tundra and create a sense of community in a society that had become diffuse.

So much, after all, is "on the brink of being lost," in the words of Mrs. Lorraine Koranda, a former teacher at the University of Alaska who has been recording Eskimo songs and customs since 1950. One of her recordings is of Chief John Oolanda of King Island in the Bering Strait, who, in a message to his relatives at Point Barrow on the mainland, intones a eulogy for himself and his way of life. His faltering words hint at a resilience of traditional values which may help to explain why the tape-recording fad has captured the Eskimos' imagination. Chief Oolanda's message is brief:

"I am sending greetings to the families of Kunaluk, Kokokruk, Kunungowruk, and Koonookyak. I have traced my ancestry and yours and found that I am related to all you men I mentioned.

"I am old now, and I do not believe I will see you again in this life. Someday we will meet somewhere else—out of the reality of this land—in a place that is not here on earth.

"I believe in God and with thoughts of Him I pray to you. I pray that you will have great success in your whaling. I pray that you will live the ways God wants you to. Then He will bless you with whales.

"Everyone who was born on the island is well. The aged ones are gone now. I had known them since they were children. I am eighty-one years of age now. My body is lessening in strength as I grow old. My friends, every day God comes nearer to me and I trust He will be here soon. Do not forget God.

"Always be thankful when you catch whales."

Seldom has a society had the good fortune of enjoying its own anthropology; even while it lives it.

Stan Steiner is currently at work on a novel about American Indians. His most recent book, Last Horse, *deals with the Navajos.*

By VICTOR GRUEN

FULL SPEED AHEAD

ON A

DEAD-END ROAD

We can still save our cities (or what's left of them),

says a noted architect and planner,

but we will have to get out of the car to do it

By 1975, we are told, more than 100,000,000 vehicles will be jockeying for position on the highways. If this trend is superimposed on today's metropolitan hodgepodge, America will be faced with an absurd paradox. Having achieved the world's highest per-capita income, the majority of our people may then have to endure not only poorer standards of transportation but lower standards of living as well. If we continue full speed ahead on the dead-end road of overmotorization, as we are told to do by the experts, we will lose our cities after killing their hearts.

There is a murder plot against our highly urbanized areas. The method the killers have chosen is that of slowly poisoning the urban body by the injection of foreign particles into its blood stream in ever-increasing doses. These particles, in the form of automobiles and trucks, cannot be absorbed by the urban body, and therefore cause circulatory diseases. The plotters are assisted by fifth columnists within the city, who—by facilitating automobile traffic through the widening of streets, narrowing of sidewalks, construction of gigantic garages within the heart area, and the whole electronic hocus-pocus of signaling systems—do everything in their power to attract more and more of the foreign particles into the very heart, until the tissues and cells of this vital organism are effectively attacked and destroyed. The injection of these foreign particles not only clogs arteries and veins, but brings with it side effects that further hasten the demise of the victim: noise, danger to life and limb, and pollution of the air, to name a few.

Medical authorities and psychologists assure us that noise is not just a nuisance. It interferes with our hearing ability, it deranges our nervous systems and our minds, and it causes serious diseases—possibly even death.

The poisoning of the air we breathe in our cities is, to a surprisingly high degree, ascribable to the exhaust gases of motorized vehicles. Arthur C. Stern of the Taft Sanitary Engineering Center has predicted that it will soon be necessary for the U.S. Weather Bureau to issue daily air pollution reports, and that more and more cities will have to prohibit auto traffic on days when pollution is critical.

Noise and fumes are slow agents of death. There are, of course, much faster ones available. As Ernest Marples, British Minister of Transport, said in 1960:

When a ton of steel moving at thirty miles an hour and eleven stone (154 pounds) of flesh and bones moving at three miles an hour share the same surface, accidents must happen. And the flesh and bones can never win.

None of these ghastly facts seems to touch in the least those experts—solid, well-meaning citizens and friends (but false friends) of the city—who are unwittingly the executors of the murder plot against it. As the freeways they design become more multitracked, the minds of these experts, the "traffickists," or traffic engineers, seem to become increasingly more single-tracked. This one-track-mindedness has led to the point where they can think no longer of any mode of transportation other than private automobile and truck.

"Autosis" has become a religious cult in which, instead of the golden calf, the godly symbol is a golden Cadillac. The believers, whom for the sake of brevity I will call auto-crats, have raised their god on a high pedestal, and preach complete subjugation to the "higher mechanical being." They accept all its manifestations in the same manner in which primitive religions have accepted elemental phenomena—the sun and the rain, thunder and light-

ning—as supreme divine forces with which man cannot presume to tangle. Members of the new cult are perfectly willing to sacrifice people and cities on the altar of their god. The evangelists of the new sect have won millions of blind followers: among them are downtown merchants who are losing business and yelling for more and more parking space to house the symbols of the new divinity, as well as city administrators prescribing that every newly erected building must provide altars to automania in the form of car storage. Overwhelmed by the evangelistic fervor of the auto-crats, urban citizens submissively surrender privacy, restfulness, beauty, time, and money, in order to please the deity from Detroit.

How far automania has progressed is illustrated by a recent planning report for the rebuilding of downtown Los Angeles, which contains this remarkable statement: "The pedestrian remains as the largest single obstacle to free traffic movement." How deeply the new dogma is felt was illustrated by the remarks of the former Traffic Commissioner of New York City, T. T. Wiley, when I had the pleasure of engaging him in a debate before a New York civic organization. He tried to establish that traffic congestion was not an evil, but a highly desirable phenomenon. To prove his point he said, "No city has ever died from too much traffic, but many have deteriorated because of too little." I replied that basically I agreed with his statement, but that I had some misgivings about his terminology: traffic, in my opinion, has nothing to do with congestion—it means movement of people and goods; the aim of transportation planning should be to provide movement in the necessary quantity *and* of the highest attainable quality. Quality relates, of course, to speed and con-

venience. Inasmuch as congestion obviously implies non-movement, it is a force hostile to the flourishing of cities. If the Commissioner would rephrase his sentence to read "No city has ever died from too much and too smooth movement of people and goods, but many have deteriorated because of too little of this type of movement," I would agree wholeheartedly with his statement.

And yet the traffickist speeds happily along with his eyes glued to the automobile in front of him, watching the rearview mirror for the car behind, and looking to neither left nor right. Driven by his one-track mind and by his devout belief in the infallibility of his god (the motorcar), he proceeds with his work of destruction on a multilane approach. With a certain genius he kills several birds (not to speak of a few pedestrians) with a few well-aimed rocks. First of all, he attempts to drag to the city center as many automobiles as he can find lurking in the metropolitan region. For this purpose he constructs bridges, tunnels, and toll roads that converge from every direction like arrows to the heart. In doing so he bankrupts public transportation, which, though painfully overcrowded during rush hours, loses customers during the rest of the day. Deprived of prospective passengers—and thus of much revenue income—public transportation is forced to cut down on the quality and quantity of its services, and to curtail improvements and new investments. This makes public transportation unpopular, and as a result an additional army of automobiles streams toward the core. This kind of aggravated traffic congestion is welcomed by the traffickist since it makes the need for his services apparent to everyone. Businessmen and the general populace, cowed into submission by the monumental traffic jams, offer no further resistance; so the traffickist can now pro-

How to make a traffic jam

I have, just for the fun of it, calculated what the space requirements would be if everybody coming into Manhattan today, whether by commuter train, subway, or other means of public transportation, were forced to use a car. If 1,000,000 transit passengers were to drive in to work or to shop, they would occupy approximately 750,000 automobiles. If, having reached Manhattan, they were satisfied merely to stand still, bumper to bumper, they would cover more than 100,000,000 square feet of surface. To make space for them within the main business area of Manhattan, we not only would have to eliminate all sidewalks, but would have to demolish every last structure, and then double-deck a part of Manhattan Island now covered by office buildings, hotels, theatres, stores, etc. Inasmuch as standing still, bumper to bumper, would be a highly undesirable and fruitless activity, and as people obviously will want to move around, we will have to provide three times that space; that means we will have to build six layers of transportation area covering the entire business core. If we also desire space for taxicabs, trucks, and service vehicles, if we consider that there might be occasional accidents and stalled cars, and if we admit that it will be necessary to build some ramps, stairs, elevators, and escalators, nine levels will be required. On top of the ninth level we could construct new buildings to house the facilities which we had to demolish in order to make space for motorization.

ceed to destroy one of the most essential qualities of the city core —namely, its compactness. He proposes (and usually gets permission for) street widenings, cross-town highways, and freeway-like main arteries through the heart of the city. Once they are constructed, he is justified in pointing out that the many cars he brought in must also somehow be stored. He then proceeds to build garages and parking lots on sites where people used to live, or work, or watch theatrical performances, or otherwise engage in urban activities. Thus he loosens the fabric of the city, destroying the experience of continuity and endangering the lives and limbs of those who had felt safe at least on the sidewalks, which now become entrances and exits for the garages. The end result is that the heart of almost any American city, seen from the air, now resembles one of the bombed-out cities of Europe after the Second World War, with only isolated buildings thrusting up through a vast sea of tin automobile roofs. At this point, the traffickist's day of glory has arrived. He can proudly point out that traffic downtown is moving. He forgets to tell us that it is about the only thing which *is* moving; merchants complain that merchandise is not moving, and every movement in the field of culture, sociability, and civic endeavor has stopped.

Few in our highly efficient industrial life are permitted to get away with such bungling procedures as the traffickists engage in. Imagine, for example, what would happen to a student in a plumbers' kindergarten if he were to build an irrigation system in such a manner that water in gigantic pipes would be carried at high velocity from all directions toward one central spot, within which he would place rusty, narrow pipes crisscrossing each other; and if, furthermore, he were to propose that this inadequate internal pipe system should take care not only of irrigation

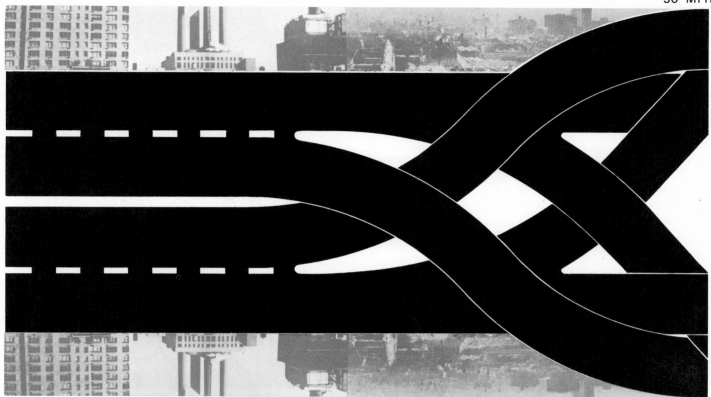

but also of drinking water, sewage, and drainage. Obviously he would be expelled from the plumbers' kindergarten, and would take up some other profession, possibly traffic engineering. In that career he would design what we are now blessed with in all our metropolitan areas: gigantic pipes in the form of highways and freeways, all converging on one little spot called downtown, there emptying into a crisscross pattern of narrow streets and roads which he would assign to the combined use of private cars, stop-and-go buses, stop-and-go taxis, trucks, pushcarts, and people. To make things more interesting, he would call on the help of other people, like double-parkers and "dig-we-must" construction crews; he would also arrange for some assorted holes in the pavement and occasional though considerable rain- and snowfall. But no bungling can discourage the traffickists. On a recent television show concerning the traffic situation in Manhattan the following statement was made by a defender of the man-made mess: "All efforts to separate machines from man are doomed to failure, because deep in human nature there is the irresistible desire of everybody to drive a car, and to drive it right to the door of the building for which he aims."

Now, if everybody were allowed to do as he wished, nobody could do what he wanted. If, for example, everybody wanted to reach, by car, the door of one of Manhattan's great department stores—let us say Macy's—that store would have to have an estimated forty thousand doors along a frontage of forty miles. Should this prove impossible, then one could, of course, construct instead a parking lot—which, however, would have to cover an area as large as that from Third to Eighth avenues, and from 30th to 38th streets. Although this might possibly satisfy Macy's, what would Gimbels say?

There comes, of course, a time when the bungling is so obvious that the citizenry starts to rebel. This is how the long-planned Broome Street Expressway in lower Manhattan was defeated. *The National Observer* of December 24, 1962, wrote under the headline LITTLE ITALY WINS STUNNING VICTORY OVER BIG HIGHWAY: "They mobilized their energies and helped defeat what one candid city official calls 'the most intractable bureaucracy known to modern man.'" The writer of the article said, "Their victory over 'City Hall' . . . would have little interest outside New York were it not for the fact that it represents the kind of struggle occurring elsewhere today in the United States—in Boston, Pittsburgh, West Palm Beach, San Francisco, Los Angeles."

Because the tremendous havoc caused in urbanized areas by the private motorcar's insatiable appetite for space is slowly being recognized, proposals for the construction of new mass transportation are, for the first time since the beginning of the century, making some headway. In San Francisco the construction of a new system costing in excess of $700,000,000 has recently been approved by the voters.

Washington, D.C., has held hearings about a new transportation system. At these hearings witness after witness has spoken out against the construction of further urban highways and freeways, and in favor of public mass transportation. A report on Bill S 3193 concerning Washington transport, printed in June, 1960, states:

It is becoming increasingly evident that any attempt to meet the area's transport needs by highways and private automobiles alone will wreck the city—it will demolish residential neighborhoods, violate parks and playgrounds, desecrate the monumental parts of the nation's capital, and remove much valuable property from the tax rolls. In any case, an all-

Eight ways to unjam the jam

Right now there is a complete disregard for gradation in urban movement, with the result that, since we do not have at our disposal a sufficient variety in types of public transportation, we are forced to use existing media in the wrong places and in the wrong manner. A new urban pattern will create a challenge to inventors, technicians, and manufacturers to supply us with new kinds of transportation carriers, and improve existing ones.

Let me try to develop schematically a *scale of gradation of movement*, as it may exist in the nation once a new urban planning philosophy starts to be implemented:

MOVEMENT AREA NO. 1: For distances of one mile and below

The most suitable means of locomotion for this movement area is traffic on foot, supplemented by various types of slow-moving carriers.

MOVEMENT AREA NO. 2: 1–2 miles

The small bus, the taxicab, and various transportation media of modest speed but continuous availability (the latter based on the moving-belt principle, with or without seats); for the transportation of goods, Carveyor belt systems.

MOVEMENT AREA NO. 3: 2–5 miles

The larger urban bus, new types of underground rapid transit; for goods, transportation by rail and by truck on special roads, etc.

MOVEMENT AREA NO. 4: 5–30 miles

Rapid transit, commuter trains, the regional bus, the private automobile; for goods, rail transportation, water transportation, trucks.

MOVEMENT AREA NO. 5: 30–60 miles

Track-bound transportation, either railroad or vehicles—already invented but still to be developed—riding on air cushions; the long-distance bus, the private automobile.

MOVEMENT AREA NO. 6: 60–400 miles

Small jet planes, new types of track-bound transportation, the private automobile; for goods, transportation by trucks, airplanes, and waterways.

MOVEMENT AREA NO. 7: Continental travel

The large jet plane, new speedy track-bound transportation; for goods, rail, planes, and waterways.

MOVEMENT AREA NO. 8: Intercontinental travel

The supersonic plane, new types of ocean liners; for goods, jet planes and shipping.

There are two types of existing transportation that I have not mentioned: the helicopter and the private plane. I believe that neither of them will be able to make a significant contribution to mass transportation, partly because of the noise caused by the helicopter and partly because both these will, in the long run, be able to function only where the airways are not too crowded.

highway solution to the area's traffic problem is a physical impossibility. Reliance on the private automobile to carry all commuters to work each day would require close to thirty freeway lanes in the north-central corridor lane alone, and would turn downtown Washington into a concrete sea of highways and parking lots. For this reason, the Washington area, like several other metropolitan areas, is showing renewed interest in public transportation. It is generally recognized that a healthy mass transportation system is essential to every metropolis.

Well, it may be generally recognized. But this does not perturb the traffickists, who have forgotten that such a thing as public mass transit even exists. They oppose all proposals for improving public transit in the nation's capital, and should they be forced to do something by public pressure, they will undertake it hesitatingly, creating some inadequate forms of transportation, which, they hope, will work unsuccessfully and thus prove their point. This attitude has moved Hillard H. Goodman, executive vice-president of the Citizen's Transit Improvement Association of Washington, to write: "The deterioration of the nation's capital will proceed at an accelerating pace if Congress and the executive branch follow the advice of highway and traffic engineers whose mission seems to be to perpetuate and increase the jobs of such engineers, who think in terms of motor vehicles instead of human beings, and who promote an endless series of projects that, instead of solving our transportation problems, greatly complicate, delay, and increase the cost of electric railroad rapid-transit construction and operation.

"In Washington as elsewhere, highway and traffic planners are dominating urban and regional planning with the result that mass transit, instead of being used to help guide the direction of public movement, patterns and growth, and the character of economic development, is expected to serve mainly as an overflow transportation facility, with rapid transit to be built only as a last resort."

Henry A. Barnes of New York, an enlightened traffic commissioner, has quite logically pointed out that the introduction of express buses on New York's parkways could take thousands of automobiles off the road, and prevent them from infiltrating Manhattan. But the traffickists told him that this was an impossible and fantastic idea. They masked themselves, this time, as friends not only of people but also of trees, plants, and flowers, and declared that parkways, as the name implied, were really parks, and were legally restricted to pleasure driving. It may be true that when parkways were first designed and constructed, their originator, Robert Moses, had a vision of families driving slowly along, stopping from time to time to picnic beside the sometimes handsomely landscaped boundaries. But Moses, who now protests against the use of parkways by buses, must have slept through the last thirty or forty years. The only place where pleasure driving still exists is in the advertisements of automobile companies, which regularly picture a single gorgeous car, utterly alone on a road that winds past luxuriant trees and meadows, or along an unpeopled seacoast or lake front. Driving an automobile may once have been a pleasure, even in urban areas. But those who use New York's parkways today are either commuters going to or from work, or people rushing to the airports. If a law permitting only pleasure driving on parkways were to be enforced, there would not be a single car left on Mr. Moses's parkways.

The traffickists' arguments against public transportation are manifold:

a) It is un-American. A true, red-blooded American is an individualist, and has a sacred right to drive his own automobile wherever he wants to go. It does not disturb the traffickist that he himself interferes with this "American freedom" by telling automobilists in which direction they may move, when they have to stop and when they may go, and that movement at those times when one most desires it consists of crawling and stopping.

b) Public transportation has been proved uneconomical, unsound, and dependent on tax subsidies, which is abhorrent to the concept of free enterprise.

c) Public transportation is unpopular; no one will ever succeed in persuading Americans to use it as long as they find it possible to steer their own cars.

These arguments, effectively supported by automobile manufacturers and highway builders, do not fail to make an impression on the public.

Interesting clues concerning the mentality of traffickists can be found in reports from the National Highway Users Conference, which took place in early March, 1962, in Washington, D. C. (One cannot get rid of the suspicion that this is a front organization for highway builders and the automobile industry.) In this conference "Freedom of Automobility" was declared. One of the speakers, William S. Canning, engineering director of the Keystone Auto Club, said that "it has become socially acceptable to oppose good roads and to damn the auto. One wonders how a movement could have arisen so suddenly in America, where the automobile has been so long a symbol of our high standard of living." Mr. Canning concluded that two persons were primarily responsible for the growth of this movement: "Messrs. Lewis Mumford and Victor Gruen." The conference then expressed special displeasure at the fact that there are people who now suggest there might be an alternative means of transportation for urban areas—such as rapid transit and other kinds of mass transportation.

The nervousness that hovered over the entire Highway Users Conference was probably justified. In spite of the fact that mass transportation was declared quite dead some time ago by traffickists and their friends, it is still quite alive. Americans do use public transportation if it is convenient, speedy, and competitively priced. For example, they use to an ever-increasing degree the airplane; they are using to a surprisingly high degree—and in spite of combined attacks—commuter trains and rapid-transit systems in our most urbanized cities (not to mention the fact that everyone, even the most ardent traffickist, uses public transportation in the form of elevators to get to his office or apartment).

As far as the question of subsidy for public transportation is concerned, it may be worthwhile to take a hard look at the public cost of private transport. Private automobile transport is subsidized to a higher degree than we ever have subsidized railways, subways, buses, or airlines. It is subsidized out of tax moneys through the construction of roads, highways, freeways, and overpasses (after the land is first acquired for them with public funds). It is subsidized by the tremendous police force needed to keep private transportation going, by the construction and operation of signaling systems, and by the construction of public garages or, where those do not exist in sufficient number, by providing—mostly free of charge—public streets and highways as stableyards for automobiles.

I am not in principle opposed to subsidy for private automobile transportation, but I feel strongly that subsidy for mass transportation—to a far greater extent than has been forthcoming anywhere up to now—is in order. Mass transportation is a public service needed for urban health, just as is a sewerage system, a street-cleaning system, or a police force. Public subsidy should be used to obtain the best possible urban transportation system for people and goods; one that will not interfere with economic and human values of the city. As far as the hearts of our cities and surrounding urbanized areas are concerned, it can be proved that an optimal system would have to be based almost wholly on mass-transportation instruments and media, with individualized transportation playing a very minor role.

Unfortunately, the resistance to destruction of the city through assault by surface mechanized traffic is still weak, and word of it has not reached the ears of those who are in charge of the fate of our cities. The 26th World Congress on Housing and Planning, which assembled in Paris in September, 1962, was under the spell of traffickist sentiment. Robert Bradbury, director of housing in Liverpool, England, remarked (I hope with tongue in cheek), "Traffic is the life stream of the twentieth century. It is a sign of success and prosperity. After all, what is a pedestrian? He is a man who has two cars, one being driven by his wife, the other by one of his children."

The Congress moved that maximum city populations in future should be held to 700,000, as in cities of this size it would be possible to arrive at reasonable automobile traffic arrangements. Thus we have—alas and alack—come to the point where the automobile will dictate the size of our cities. We will have to demolish Paris, London, Berlin, and Vienna—and Chicago, Philadelphia, and Boston. We will have to divide New York City into approximately a dozen cities, and we will have to proceed similarly with all other large cities in the world. What the Congress has decided about the fate of the inhabitants of these cities —whether they should be killed outright or deported—I wasn't able to learn. But I do know that cutting down the size of all cities to 700,000 would not solve the problems that automobiles create in them. As long as we follow the traffickist's high-speed ride on a dead-end road, we will not arrive at anything that deserves to call itself a city.

*Victor Gruen, the architect and city planner, is known to our readers for his intelligent proposal for a 1964 World's Fair that could be converted into a permanent community (*HORIZON, *May, 1960). This article is from his forthcoming book* The Heart of Our Cities, *to be published by Simon & Schuster later this summer. In it he analyzes the problems of American cities and makes suggestions for their improvement based on his wide practical experience.*

*The god of maize, elaborately crowned with flowers and a bat's head, is repre-
sented on this Mexican pottery urn. Although it looks baroque, it was made
by a Zapotec artist at least five hundred years before the Spaniards arrived.*

REDISCOVERING
AMERICA

By ALFRED KIDDER II

The long-buried past of preconquest America

is only beginning to emerge:

it is more brilliant, more complex, and more

ancient than anyone had dreamed

Serious archaeology—as opposed to the looting of tombs for gold and fine sculpture—has been going on in Latin America only since the 1890's. Long before then, of course, most of the educated world had heard of Montezuma, the tragic king of the Aztecs, of the splendor of the Inca cities conquered by Pizarro, and of the Maya and their mysterious hieroglyphs. Some of the great sites had always been known —Chichén Itzá, Mayapán, Uxmal, Tikal, Copán, Mitla, Monte Alban—but no one had tried to free the magnificent buildings from the jungle which had reclaimed them. Others, like Machu Picchu, high in the Andes, and Bonampak, now famous for its brilliant murals, were unknown to anyone except possibly a few Indians. In 1910 the compilers of the *Encyclopedia Britannica* knew only enough about the Maya to give them one brief paragraph and to observe: "As a science, the archaeology of Central America has scarcely yet emerged from its infancy."

Now, fifty years later, the archaeology of all the Americas has begun to come of age. So many new and important discoveries have been made, especially since World War II, that we are able to speak fairly confidently about how the native American civilizations came into being. When the Spaniards and Portuguese arrived in the sixteenth century, two of these civilizations still flourished: that of the Aztecs and their neighbors in Mexico and Central America, and that of the Incas in Peru and parts of Bolivia and Ecuador. For some time it was supposed that these represented the pinnacle of human attainment in preconquest America. Now we know that the Aztecs and Incas were latecomers, preceded by peoples far more inventive than

they. We also know that the two areas in which they lived —one extending from Central Mexico through what is now Guatemala into Honduras, and the other in the Central Andean region of South America—were from the beginning the centers of true cultural achievement. The Indian ways of life everywhere else in the Western Hemisphere were marginal to the life of the two great centers which archaeologists have come to call "nuclear America." We are now beginning to learn something about the relationship between these two nuclear areas, as well as their influence on the marginal areas. Evidence on this question and many others has accumulated so fast in the past twenty-five years that the history of preconquest America has almost been re-written.

One of the many causes of this advance was the invention, in 1947, of the carbon-14 method of estimating dates. A by-product of atomic research, it is based on the discovery that all living things contain a definite amount of radioactive carbon which, upon death, begins to diminish at a regular rate. Measuring the amount of this substance still present in organic material can supply, or at least suggest, a date. It works only with what was once alive—burned bones, cloth, charred wood—but the dates of stone tools or pottery

TEXT CONTINUED ON PAGE 78

This sensuously carved basalt head, nine feet high, is a spectacular example of the art of the Olmecs, the talented people who built what may have been the first civilization of Mexico. For centuries the head lay half-buried in a ravine at San Lorenzo. In 1946 it was excavated and has since been moved—despite its fourteen tons—to the Jalapa Museum.

74

LEE BOLTIN—SKIRA

These Olmec figurines, seen below just as they were discovered and, at left, as they were reassembled for the National Anthropological Museum in Mexico City, were found at La Venta, Mexico, in 1955. They are thought to date back to before 200 B.C.; their meaning can only be guessed at. Are they celebrating a rite, or holding a trial or a council of war? Fifteen of the figurines are jade; the sixteenth (center) is of serpentine. Perhaps it represents a priest, perhaps a sacrificial victim.

PHILIP DRUCKER © NATIONAL GEOGRAPHIC SOCIETY

I.N.A.H., MEXICO CITY

An Aztec legend that survived the Spanish conquest relates that Teotihuacán was a meeting place for the gods and that the Pyramid of the Sun (center) was built by a race of giants. The site, which is the largest in Mexico and is now the scene of full-scale excavations, was inhabited from about 500 B.C. to A.D. 850 by a civilized and independent people known to us simply as the Teotihuacanos. Their well-planned city, long thought to be the work of the Toltecs or Aztecs, was rich in art, some of which is being recovered. The par-

TEXT CONTINUED FROM PAGE 74

or works of art can be generally determined from the age of the organic remains found near them. In addition to this limitation the margin of error is wide—at least a century, sometimes as much as a millennium. But the technique has proved to be enormously useful in establishing basic chronologies.

To begin with, how long have the Indians been in America? Until quite recently this has been a debatable question, although it has been known since the mid 1920's that they had reached the high plains east of the Rocky Mountains by the end of the last ice age, some ten thousand years ago. It is now widely accepted that there were people in North America at least twelve thousand years ago and probably long before that—even as long ago as thirty or forty thousand years. It is also quite certain that they came here from Asia over a wide bridge of land between Siberia and Alaska at what is now Bering Strait. These people were hunters and gatherers of wild plants. They migrated slowly across North America and obviously proceeded southward. Obviously—but until recently there has been scarcely any evidence of the existence of Stone Age hunters south of the United States. Then, in the late 1930's, Dr. Junius Bird of the American Museum of Natural History found two caves in southern Chile, just north of the Strait of Magellan, which had been occupied by successive groups of hunters. The most ancient group was represented by stone spear

points and other tools found with the bones of an extinct species of horse. Dr. Bird estimated their dates as between 7000 and 9000 B.C. After the war this estimate was confirmed by means of carbon-14 tests. The discovery indicated, of course, that Indians must have been present to the north of Chile at an even earlier date, although probably not in large numbers; they were more likely small nomadic bands of no more than a few dozen people. (We know from studying the habits of more recent hunters and gatherers that such people are often nomadic and do not live permanently in large concentrations.)

Since these Chilean discoveries, more evidence of the presence of hunters has come to light, though less in South than in North America. Early sites are usually small and hard to find, and in the nuclear areas such simple and unspectacular remains are overshadowed by the ruins of much richer and more elaborate cultures. Nevertheless, large stone spear points with a radiocarbon date of about 7000 B.C. were found with the bones of mammoths in the Valley of Mexico and in northern Venezuela. Crude spear points found in northwestern Argentina date from around 6000 B.C. The Central Andes have yielded few early remains, but enough to show that Stone Age hunters lived in the Peruvian and Bolivian highlands. Spear points excavated in Ecuador bear a type of longitudinal fluting characteristic of points

tially excavated area at the base of the Pyramid of the Sun is in the "Street of the Dead," once the main avenue. Many new frescoes have turned up in the buildings along this avenue. The one at left, dated to about A.D. 500, shows a fish and a red jaguar. On the balustrade of a temple stairway (right) is the fierce-looking head of the plumed serpent Quetzalcoatl, one of the chief deities of Teotihuacán. Both the jaguar and the plumed serpent were divine symbols for many of the ancient American peoples, from Mexico to Peru.

found in the western plains of the United States, where they date from about 12,000 to 9,000 B.C. With the increasing interest in this early hunting stage of history, many more sites are sure to be found and excavated, although it will be difficult, perhaps impossible, to discover any in the tropical rain forests. There the heavy growth of the jungle and the changing of stream beds over the millennia make the search for small sites difficult. Also, the lack of stone in these areas means that early inhabitants had to depend on perishable materials for tools, and thus they left few relics behind them until they began to use pottery in later ages. This is unfortunate, for a study of the ways in which the Indians adapted to tropical forest life, as they moved slowly southward, would be of the greatest interest.

It is clear nonetheless that man has been in Latin America for a very respectable length of time—long enough to adapt himself to the drastically differing altitudes and climates he encountered in that vast area. Eventually, of course, he took the first step toward civilization and began to farm, though how and where and when are questions we are only beginning to answer. In the history of American archaeology there have been few serious scholars who did not believe that the American Indians invented their own agriculture, quite independently of influences from the Old World. This conviction was based on the fact that all the basic crops cultivated by the Indian are American in origin. None of

the staples of the Old World, such as wheat, barley, and rye, were known in this hemisphere. Until very lately, however, we did not know where domestication of many plants first took place or the order in which they were domesticated. The potato, for example, was never grown anywhere but in the Andean highlands until the Spaniards arrived. Yet we will probably never be able to find out when men first began to grow potatoes because the climate of the Peruvian and Bolivian highlands is not dry enough to preserve the tubers. Corn, on the other hand, occurs in many places, but only recently have we learned where it came from. For a long time it was thought to have been derived from a wild grass called *teocintli*, which grows in Mexico. Genetic experiments showed that this was untrue. But, when very early corn was found in a cave in New Mexico, and still earlier corn in Mexico, it became apparent that at least the theory of Mexican origin was correct.

The excavations that produced the Mexican evidence were carried out by Richard S. MacNeish in the state of Puebla in the Tehuacán Valley, southeast of Mexico City. Sponsored by the Robert S. Peabody Foundation of Phillips Academy at Andover, Massachusetts, it is one of the most important projects in the history of American archaeology, for it has done more than any other single campaign to close the gap in our knowledge of the period between the early hunters and the farming villagers whose way of life devel-

UNIVERSITY MUSEUM, UNIV. OF PA.; BELOW: LEE BOLTIN

ABOVE: *When archaeologists from the University of Pennsylvania began work at Tikal in 1956, the vast Maya site had all but vanished into the jungle. "Temple I" (foreground) was among the highest to be cleared.* BELOW: *One of the many treasures to turn up at Tikal was the "Red Stela." It was probably sacred; yet it had been deliberately defaced, perhaps by a rebellious mob.*

oped into the Classic civilizations of Mexico. In this one small region a span of more than eight thousand years of human development is becoming visible.

The work at Tehuacán has been carried out on about ten sites, five of them being dry caves. Thousands of bits of imperishable materials have come to light, and a wealth of perishable remains of food plants, baskets, and netting. MacNeish has outlined seven developmental stages, running from about 7000 B.C. to A.D. 1200. In the earliest stage the population was very small and the people lived by hunting and trapping as well as by gathering wild plants. By 6000 B.C., they had squashes and chili peppers, representing what MacNeish calls early attempts at rudimentary agriculture. As time passed, these people depended more and more on farming. Corn of a very primitive type appears possibly as early as 5000 B.C., followed by beans and gourds. Thus the basic trilogy of American Indian agriculture—corn, beans, and squashes—must have been established in Mexico by at least 3000 B.C.

The same momentous transition from hunting to farming took place in Peru, but at a later date. In 1946 at Huaca

RIGHT: *"Temple I" has now been divested of its greenery and repaired. Rising to a majestic 229 feet, it dominates the Grand Plaza at Tikal.*
BELOW: *This ceramic vessel, bearing a date equivalent to A.D. 754, survived in a grave at Altar de Sacrificios near Tikal. It shows a lithe dancer wearing the skin of a jaguar; the animal's head serves as a head-dress, while the paws are mittens.*

Prieta, near the mouth of the Chicama River in northern Peru, Dr. Bird excavated a large mound which contained quantities of ash, firestones, sea-urchin spines, and fishbones, along with baskets, bits of cotton cloth, and simple stone tools. The people whose way of life is made evident by these modest objects lived in underground houses on this site from 2500 to 1200 B.C. They had no pottery and did no hunting but depended instead on the sea for fish and sea urchins and on the lagoons for the roots of rushes. They also raised cotton, squashes, gourds, chili peppers, and perhaps some other local plants. Dozens of sites like Huaca Prieta are now known. The people who lived in them did not all depend so completely on the sea and lagoons, but all of them farmed, some perhaps as early as 4000 B.C. But not until 1400 B.C. did they have corn. And grain is the basis of a real agriculture, capable of supporting a specialized civilization. Cotton that can be spun poses a problem of origin that is still unsolved. This is too lengthy and technical to be discussed here, but it involves the question of the possible transoceanic introduction, either naturally or through human agency, of a long-staple species that is thought to have been hybridized

with wild Peruvian unlinted cotton. Cotton is apparently earlier in Peru than in Mexico.

The development of pottery—another of the major steps toward civilized life—for the most part remains a mystery. It appears in Mexico about 2500 B.C., but it is not possible to say whether it was invented there or not. There is some evidence that in North America the earliest wares may be of Asiatic inspiration. There is even stronger evidence that this was the case on the west coast of South America. In southern Ecuador, not far from the city of Guayaquil, the late Emilio Estrada, working with Clifford Evans and Betty Meggers of the Smithsonian Institution, found unpainted pottery that has all the earmarks of Japanese influence. The fragments, carbon dated to around 2500 B.C., were decorated by incision—impression with a sharp instrument on the wet surface of the clay—in a way that exactly resembles the decoration of pottery in Japan during the same period. The designs, though very simple, are not to be found anywhere else in this hemisphere. Clifford Evans believes a Japanese ship must have come ashore on the Ecuadorian coast in the middle of the third millennium B.C. Ocean currents

While the Incas left behind at least some oral historic evidence, their precursors in Peru are known to us only by a few ingenious works of art. The cloth warrior above, embroidered in vivid colors on a cloak used as a mummy wrapping, was found, along with many other such textiles, miraculously well-preserved in a two-thousand-year-old necropolis on the Paracas peninsula of Peru. The ceramic at left, made in a distinctive Peruvian style called Recuay, has been tentatively dated to about A.D. 700. The wide-eyed figure seated in the middle may represent a chief, for he is attended by five diminutive women who offer him drinking cups, and by four men holding a canopy.

would make such landfalls quite possible, and the southern Ecuadorian coast is precisely where one would expect them to occur.

These new sites—the hunters' caves in Chile, Tehuacán in central Mexico, Huaca Prieta in Peru, and the site near Guayaquil in Ecuador—have substantially broadened our knowledge of early American man. The gaps in that knowledge are still immense, but a sound beginning has at least been made. One of the questions that motivate the study is whether early man, in what must have been the comparative isolation of America, behaved like his Middle Eastern counterpart, first making his way as a hunter, then learning to farm, then settling down to village life, and—sometimes —progressing from there to urban civilization. If so, did he do all this by his own ingenuity, without help from abroad? The answer is not yet certain, but it would appear to be yes.

"Formative" is a term we apply to that stage of life in Mexico and Peru when a stable agriculture had been achieved that enabled villages to exist and populations to grow. This occurred between 1500 and 500 B.C. when, technically and socially, the great Classic civilizations of the Americas were being forged. Five thousand years separate the earliest beginnings of agriculture in Mexico from the Formative stage. In Peru, which got a later start, not so much time was needed—only six hundred years if this is calculated from the introduction of corn. The reason for such an accelerated pace in Peru must lie in its geographical differences from Mexico. In Peru, with its small coastal valleys separated by miles of desert, arable land is limited. Any sort of really productive agriculture requires irrigation; and once the valleys began to be exploited with canals, their potential was realized very quickly.

The Formative period is by now one of the better known eras of Latin American history before the conquest. There has not been much recent field work on it in Peru; in Mexico and the Maya area, on the other hand, there has been a lot of work on major ruins whose histories begin in Formative times. There have also been recent campaigns in Chiapas, the Gulf Coast, and western Guatemala. The results are still largely unpublished. Perhaps the most surprising discovery is evidence that there was contact by sea between the Pacific coast of Guatemala and the coast of Ecuador about 1000 B.C. This maritime connection may have had some influence on the early art of the Mexican and Maya areas, for it is thought that certain female figurines may have been brought there from Ecuador.

The most interesting civilization of this Formative period —and the most controversial—is that of the Olmecs, or "rubber people," as the Aztecs were to name them centuries later. They must have been an extraordinary people; indeed, some think they built the mother civilization of Mexico and Central America. Their art, striking and powerful, consists mainly of stone sculptures, with emphasis on the jaguar

TEXT CONTINUED ON PAGE 86

Machu Picchu (above), set on a 6,750-foot peak in the Peruvian Andes—unnoticed by the Spanish conquerors—was unknown to archaeologists until 1910. The "Gateway of the Sun" (below) at Tiahuanaco in Bolivia is the relic of a little-known culture that flourished about A.D. 500 and expanded into Peru long before the Inca warriors made themselves masters of the Andes.

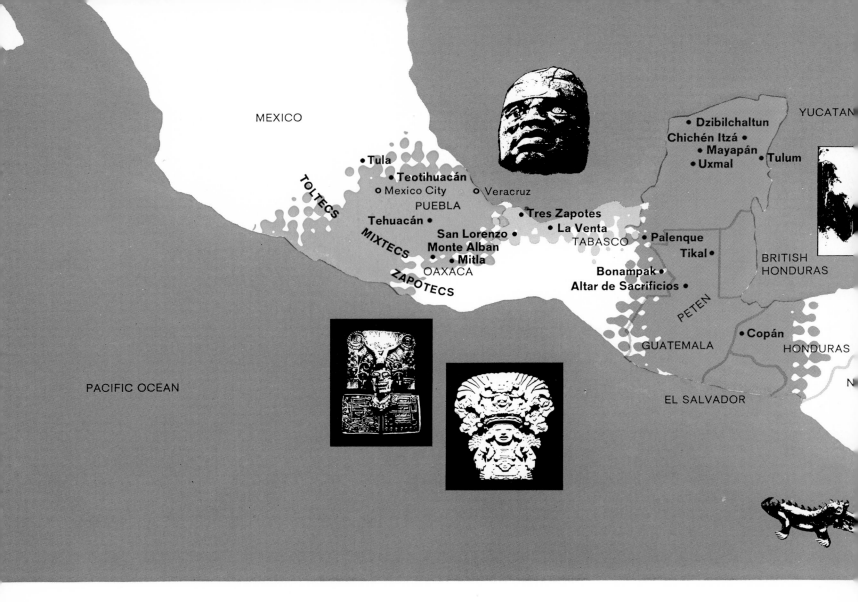

MEXICO

• Tula
• Teotihuacán
○ Mexico City   ○ Veracruz
PUEBLA
Tehuacán •
          • San Lorenzo
          Monte Alban
            • Mitla
OAXACA

TOLTECS

MIXTECS

ZAPOTECS

• Tres Zapotes
• La Venta
TABASCO
            • Palenque
            Tikal •
Bonampak •
Altar de Sacrificios •

PETEN

• Dzibilchaltun
Chichén Itzá •
    • Mayapán
  • Uxmal   • Tulum

YUCATAN

BRITISH
HONDURAS

• Copán   HONDURAS

GUATEMALA

PACIFIC OCEAN

EL SALVADOR

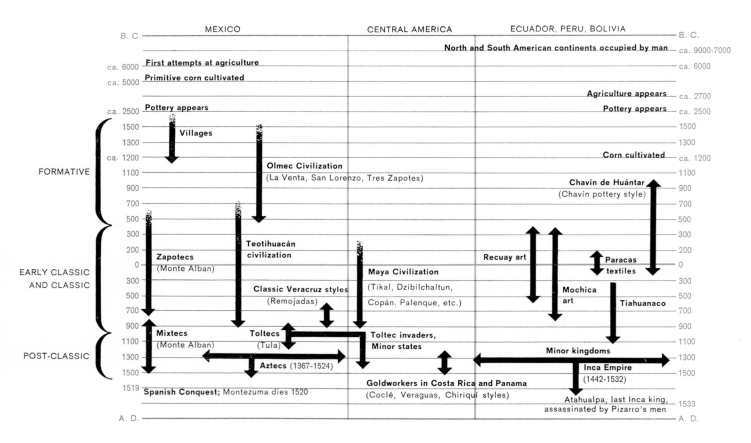

	MEXICO	CENTRAL AMERICA	ECUADOR, PERU, BOLIVIA	
B. C.				B. C.
			North and South American continents occupied by man	ca. 9000-7000
ca. 6000	First attempts at agriculture			ca. 6000
ca. 5000	Primitive corn cultivated			
			Agriculture appears	ca. 2700
ca. 2500	Pottery appears		Pottery appears	ca. 2500
1500	Villages			1500
1300				1300
ca. 1200			Corn cultivated	ca. 1200
1100	Olmec Civilization			1100
900	(La Venta, San Lorenzo, Tres Zapotes)		Chavín de Huántar	900
700			(Chavín pottery style)	700
500				500
300	Teotihuacán		Recuay art	300
200	civilization		Paracas	200
0	Zapotecs		textiles	0
300	(Monte Alban)	Maya Civilization	Mochica	300
500	Classic Veracruz styles	(Tikal, Dzibilchaltun,	art	500
700	(Remojadas)	Copán, Palenque, etc.)	Tiahuanaco	700
900	Mixtecs	Toltecs	Toltec invaders,	900
1100	(Monte Alban)	(Tula)	Minor states	Minor kingdoms	1100
1300	Aztecs (1367-1524)			1300
1500			Inca Empire	1500
1519	Spanish Conquest; Montezuma dies 1520	Goldworkers in Costa Rica and Panama	(1442-1532)	
		(Coclé, Veraguas, Chiriquí styles)	Atahualpa, last Inca king,	1533
			assassinated by Pizarro's men	
A. D.				A. D.

FORMATIVE

EARLY CLASSIC
AND CLASSIC

POST-CLASSIC

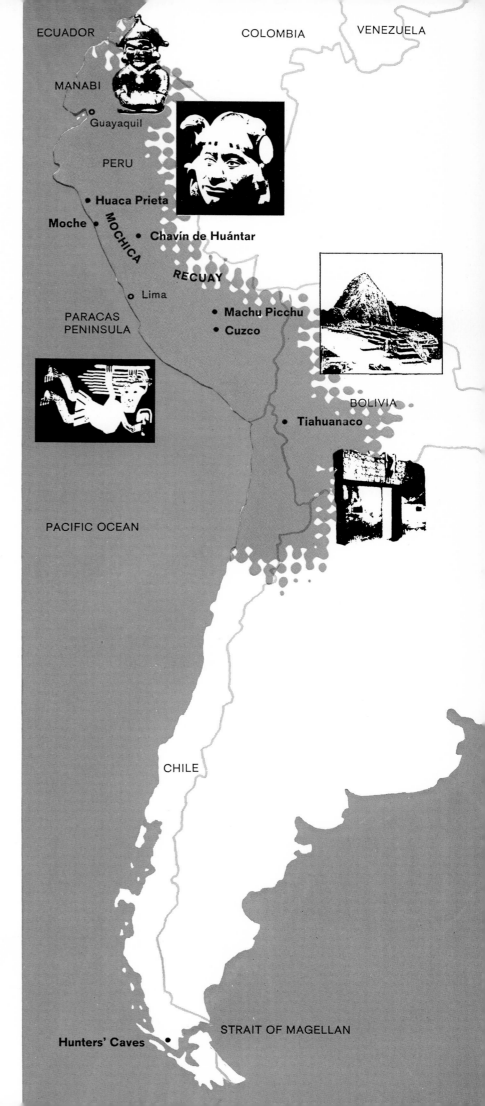

ECUADOR

MANABI

o
Guayaquil

PERU

• Huaca Prieta

Moche •

MOCHICA

• Chavín de Huántar

RECUAY

o Lima

PARACAS
PENINSULA

• Machu Picchu

• Cuzco

PACIFIC OCEAN

COLOMBIA

VENEZUELA

BOLIVIA

• Tiahuanaco

CHILE

STRAIT OF MAGELLAN

Hunters' Caves •

ENINSULA

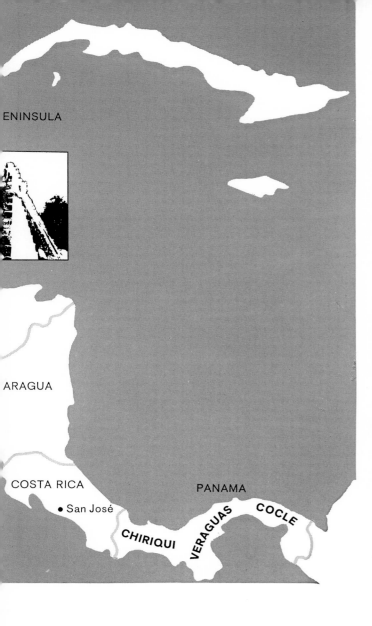

ARAGUA

COSTA RICA

• San José

PANAMA

CHIRIQUI   VERAGUAS   COCLE

EARLIEST
AMERICA

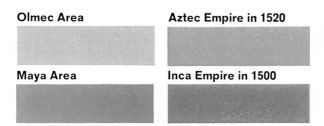

Olmec Area

Aztec Empire in 1520

Maya Area

Inca Empire in 1500

The pottery model of a house (above), found recently in the Manabí province of Ecuador, looks extraordinarily like the houses of Micronesia; for example the gabled huts of the Palau islands (right). The Manabí figurine (below) also suggests an Asiatic prototype, for its pose and smile resemble that of the tenth-century Buddha from southeast Asia (bottom). The question of whether man in ancient America evolved his own culture or imported it has inspired many a wild surmise. Scholars doubt that major cultural exchanges between the hemispheres occurred, but finds such as these indicate that at least some ships from across the Pacific must have reached America.

TEXT CONTINUED FROM PAGE 83

and serpent motifs, and on combinations of feline and human elements. Such works of art were found for the most part in three ceremonial centers in southeastern Mexico—La Venta, Tres Zapotes, and San Lorenzo, cities which outstrip in size and ingenuity all others of comparable date. The gigantic stone heads left at La Venta by the Olmecs have been there for all to see for centuries, but it was only in the late 1930's that any serious notice was taken of them. Now, however, the study of this art has led to the conclusion that the Olmecs were the progenitors of civilization in Mexico.

Such a conclusion depends largely on dating. Radiocarbon dates of 800 to 400 B.C. were arrived at by analyzing charcoal found at La Venta, the ceremonial center in Tabasco that has produced so much spectacular Olmec art. Some scholars question these dates, not because they doubt the efficacy of the radiocarbon method, but because they do not believe that the charcoal is really contemporaneous with the monuments and carved jade—definitely Olmec—from the same site. It is a question that will require a great deal more field work before it is solved. A reliable dating of the Olmec civilization would not only tell us much about early Mexico but also about early Peru. Some archaeologists believe that Olmec influences—transported through sea trade —were basic to the great art style of Chavín in northern Peru, where there was also a jaguar god.

Whether or not the Olmec culture was the basis of the Classic civilizations, they were coming into being architecturally and artistically a century or two before the beginning of the Christian Era. The great independent centers of Teotihuacán in central Mexico and Monte Alban in the south were taking shape. To the south of them, in what is now Guatemala, the Maya were just beginning to build on a large scale. In northern Peru a people whom we call Mochica, but whose ancient name we do not even know, had already developed one of the great pottery styles of ancient America. In central Peru, on the Paracas peninsula, a little-known people had developed an art and a style of weaving which, according to a modern art critic, has "few parallels anywhere in the world for fineness and intricacy." There is still much to be learned about this early classic stage, which is probably the most impressive period in ancient American history. The many archaeological projects under way are yielding spectacular results.

One of the largest of these projects is the full-scale excavation the Mexican government has begun, under the direction of Ignacio Bernal, at Teotihuacán, close to Mexico City. Teotihuacán has long been famous for its twin pyramids "of the Sun and the Moon," but now a great quantity of new sculpture and many new frescoes have been recovered there. In addition, Teotihuacán appears to have been a true city with a large permanent population, not merely a ceremonial center. If so, it was without doubt one of the biggest cities of preconquest Mexico and of the entire ancient American world.

Tikal, a notable Maya site in the jungle of the Petén district in northeastern Guatemala, has been under excavation by the University of Pennsylvania Museum since 1957. Originally directed by Edwin Shook, the project is now under the joint supervision of Aubrey Trik and William R. Coe. Tikal is the largest Maya ruin known—at least it has the largest temples. Five of these rise above the jungle to heights of more than two hundred feet. Archaeologists have mapped six square miles of the site without reaching all the outer limits.

Our knowledge of the Maya is probably as advanced as that of any ancient American culture, but innumerable questions remain unanswered. We know that the Maya flourished in what is now Guatemala, western Honduras, and the Mexican state of Yucatán from about A.D. 100 to 900. But where did these remarkable people come from? What was their way of life in the beginning? What outside influences, if any, did they undergo? Can Tikal, or any of the other Maya sites, be properly termed "cities"? Or were they ceremonial centers which housed only the priestly class? No one can give definite answers.

Another problem that for many years has been the subject of controversy among Maya scholars is how to correlate the Maya and Christian calendars. The glyphs they carved on their stelae are often dates—indeed, the dates are all that we are as yet able to decipher. By the time the Spaniards arrived in the sixteenth century, the Maya of Yucatán were no longer recording dates in the old way and could give their conquerors only a sketchy idea of what the calendrical glyphs signified. They could identify a date but only within a limited cycle of time, exactly as though we were told that it was July 1, 64—without the century. While we count time in units of one hundred years, the basic unit of the Maya is about two hundred and sixty years. Though scholars are perfectly able to read the glyphs expressing the date of a day and the name of a month, they are then faced with the choice of placing it in any one of three or four Maya "centuries." The only way this problem could be solved was to determine accurately the Christian date of some object which had already been dated by the Maya system. Carbon dating provided a method of doing this, except that nearly all Maya dates are carved in stone and thus cannot be tested. However, at Tikal there are a number of standing temples with large, beautifully carved wooden lintels, some of which are dated. Wood from uncarved beams, assumed to be contemporaneous with the carved ones, was taken from several temples; and a long series of carbon tests was run on both at the University of Pennsylvania laboratory. The result was a consistent pattern of dates that indicates which of the Maya centuries is the correct one to choose in correlating the two calendars. Thus one problem has been solved.

The question of whether Tikal was really a city with a stable population has been answered by excavating small

TEXT CONTINUED ON PAGE 93

Scientists and workmen sift through the dust of a cave at Tehuacán in southern Mexico to find any sign of prehistoric life—a corncob, a dried seed, a bit of cloth. Embedded in the strata of this cave floor is a long sequence of evidence showing how man gradually gave up hunting and learned to farm.

TREASURES

OF

ANCIENT

AMERICAN

ART

In a Costa Rican bank vault Skira author Samuel Lothrop (left) and bank officials examine new art treasures, among them the six-inch crocodile shown in our portfolio.

Our store of ancient American art grows richer each year as the archaeologist labors; meanwhile, unfortunately, the looter loots. Many of the objects in these pages were lifted from the earth with care, meticulously studied, and then lovingly catalogued for some national museum. Others were merely lifted—usually from an ancient tomb—and put on the art market, whence they passed into a collector's hands. Thus has the beautiful art of preconquest America accumulated for our pleasure, much as Egyptian antiquities did in an earlier generation. But it is only in recent years that a body of knowledge has been growing apace with this newly discovered art. The anthropologist and the archaeologist try to reconstruct a history or at least a context for each new find. The art historian and critic, who is a latecomer to the field, tries to elucidate the beauties of this native but alien tradition and to organize the proliferating styles into some coherent pattern.

With this latter purpose in mind, the editors of HORIZON asked Albert Skira, the Swiss publisher, to prepare a new book. *Treasures of Ancient America,* which is to be published later this year, will contain photographs of works in numerous collections, from Mexico to Peru, from Los Angeles to Vienna. Many of these art objects have never been reproduced before. The author of the book is Dr. Samuel Lothrop of the Peabody Museum at Harvard; the photographer is Lee Boltin. HORIZON is pleased to present in the following portfolio a selection of some of the pictures which will appear in *Treasures of Ancient America.*

The ceramic jar seen on the opposite page was made by a gifted Mochica potter, probably before A.D. 600. The Mochica, whose ancient name is not known, were a warlike people of northwest Peru. The particularity and realism of this face suggests that it is a portrait. The hat, for no good reason that we know, is a splendid pair of birds. The piece belongs to the National Anthropological Museum at Lima.

The gold pendant on page 90 looks massive but is less than five inches high. It represents a Mexican god of death, with fleshless jaws and staring eyes. Made by a Mixtec artist around A.D. 1400, it is now in the museum at Oaxaca, Mexico. The Mixtecs, who lived at Monte Alban from about A.D. 900 onward, never fell under Aztec domination.

Another gold pendant (page 91) represents a crocodile, with bells for eyes, holding a man in its mouth (only the feet can be seen protruding). It turned up last year in a graveyard in Costa Rica, along with a hoard of similar figurines. This one resembles pieces cast in the Veraguas, Coclé, and Chiriquí styles of Panama and may date from the fifteenth century A.D. The Costa Rican government has taken charge of the new treasures; they are in a bank vault in San José.

The superb embroidery on the last page of the portfolio was found on the Paracas peninsula of Peru and is now in the National Anthropological Museum at Lima. Its brilliant colors belie its age: it may have been made before Augustus Caesar died. The creature it depicts could have come from Edward Lear; it is a combination of owl and pussycat—and a pregnant one, at that. Inside its belly is a cat-demon, with a conveniently angular tail, and inside *that* cat-demon is an identical, but smaller, cat-demon.

MOCHICA PORTRAIT JAR, PROBABLY BEFORE A.D. 600

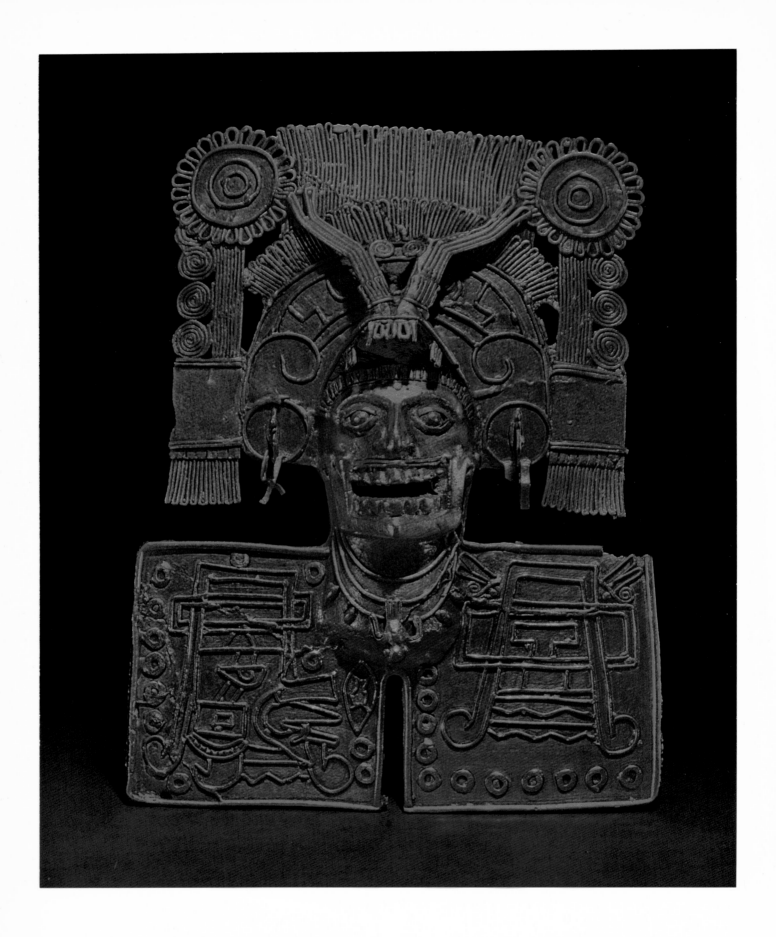

GOLD PENDANT REPRESENTING THE GOD OF DEATH, FOURTEENTH OR FIFTEENTH CENTURY A.D.

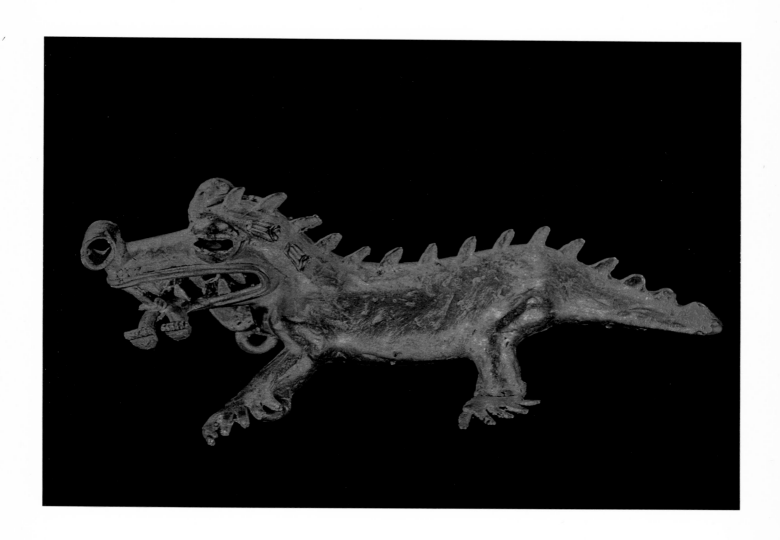

GOLD PENDANT SHAPED AS A CROCODILE, FOURTEENTH OR FIFTEENTH CENTURY A.D.

EMBROIDERED DETAIL FROM A PARACAS MANTLE, PROBABLY MADE BETWEEN 100 B.C. AND A.D. 100

TEXT CONTINUED FROM PAGE 87

mounds and houses; it appears that it was. Tikal, obviously of enormous prestige and importance in the region, seems to have had a citizenry of full-time administrators, architects, sculptors, jade carvers, potters, and many others to supply the needs of the large priestly hierarchy that ruled the city. These urbanites, who must have lived close to the center of Tikal, were supported by farmers living farther away.

But the most perplexing problem concerning the Maya is how to explain the sudden breakdown of their society and the subsequent gradual abandonment of the whole lowland area, with its hundreds of important sites, at the base of the Yucatán peninsula. In about A.D. 900 the elaborate Maya calendar ceases. There are no large-scale building projects after that date. The illiterate populace was evidently without the leadership of their priests, for they set up pieces of broken monuments with carved inscriptions in meaningless ways. Many explanations have been advanced, but the most likely one is that the people revolted and overthrew their priesthood. As I have written elsewhere, "During the late Classic years, the tempo of building and of erecting stelae was greatly accelerated. One feels that these projects, all with their attendant artistic embellishment, is at once evidence of pressure on the people and on the priests. Once embarked on a course of worship and propitiation involving great monuments and the work of numerous craftsmen and artists, no leader . . . could afford to relax. Furthermore . . . the priesthood could not afford mistakes. They were bound to have explanations and excuses ready in case their predictions, based on their almanacs, proved false. They could either blame the gods, themselves, or the people, and it is not likely that the latter were often spared . . .

"It is not difficult to imagine that in a situation of this kind enough mistakes could lead a people under tension to revolt. Most archaeologists now believe that the final collapse of the most highly organized and artistically and intellectually developed stage of Maya civilization was brought about by such a revolt against their leaders. Other explanations have been suggested chiefly having to do with the difficulties of a large population practicing agriculture in the tropical forest. The two explanations may well be connected, for if a cycle of drought, upsetting the delicate balance of success and failure of the crops, had coincided with priestly predictions of good times and continued demand for labor, the people might have overcome their awe and destroyed the hierarchy in a day. No matter how one may regard these attempts at explanation, the fact remains that Maya civilization abruptly collapsed at just the point when tension may be inferred to have been at a high level. With the loss of control by the priestly class, the great ceremonial centers fell into disrepair, art was no longer created, and the population both dispersed and decreased." Some sites, including Tikal, continued to be occupied for an as yet undetermined length of time. But the Classic period was at an end.

Tikal is by no means the only major Maya ruin to have been excavated in recent years. The Carnegie Institution of Washington has finished a complete study of the walled city of Mayapán, one of the warring cities of the post-Classic period. Tulane University has also been engaged on a long-term project in Yucatán at the enormous site of Dzibilchaltun, which was occupied continuously from perhaps as early as 500 B.C. until the Spanish conquest. Harvard University has finished important excavations in British Honduras, is now winding up several years of work at Altar de Sacrificios, south of Tikal, and will begin a new campaign at Seibal.

In recent years there have been considerably more large-scale excavations in the Maya area than in Peru and Bolivia. An exception is the extensive campaign at Tiahuanaco, in highland Bolivia, being conducted by the Bolivian government. Preliminary reports indicate that the chronology of this important site will be lengthened and that much new information on its architecture will be forthcoming. Tiahuanaco was an important center long before the Incas came, and its artistic influence is evident throughout the Central Andes.

The most important developments in South America of late have been in Ecuador. In addition to their discovery of very early contacts between Ecuador and Japan, the Estrada-Evans-Meggers team found a culture on the coast of Ecuador that had maritime contacts with Mexico in Classic times. And about 200 B.C. Ecuador apparently had another visit from Asia. At that time, to quote Evans, "a unique ritual complex makes its appearance, neck-rests, models of houses with saddle roofs and columns, realistic figurines with legs folded one above the other, novel golf-tee earplugs, and pendants of stone and pottery fashioned in the form of a tusk." Such objects were completely unknown in the New World at that time, and there is little doubt that the arrival of a vessel from Asia is responsible for their existence. As in the case of the earlier contact, the elements of Asiatic inspiration were not long retained.

This article does not pretend to cover all the recent advances in the archaeology of Latin America. Our knowledge is constantly expanding. Less than twenty-five years ago the earliest-known cultures of Peru were the Classic ones, and the Formative period of Mexico was thought to date back only to about A.D. 300. Now, the history of man in this hemisphere has become much clearer. But many chapters of that history remain a blank, and even the well-known periods need years of field work and study. Not until we have reached a stage where *all* the evidence from a number of major sites has been obtained and studied can we say that archaeology in America has come of age.

Alfred Kidder II, the son of a pioneer in American archaeology and himself an archaeologist, is Associate Director of the University Museum at the University of Pennsylvania.

THE SOLITARY WANDERER

Often cast as the putative father of revolutionists, totalitarians, nudists, and square dancers, Jean Jacques Rousseau is now re-established in a role that is better suited to him—as prophet of man's predicament in an increasingly complex civilization

By J. CHRISTOPHER HEROLD

When, in 1778, Rousseau died at the age of sixty-six, one of the most tortured existences ever recorded came to an end. He had spent the better part of his life as a tramp. Suddenly shot to fame, he had been at the same time hunted like a criminal over the face of Europe and consulted like an oracle. He had made enemies of all his friends and had spent his final years in a state close to insanity. He had suffered from a variety of bizarre physiological complaints and from almost every conceivable form of neurosis. He had never owned a house or founded a family (he abandoned his five illegitimate children to an orphan asylum). He had been ostracized in his native land. He had published, in his lifetime, a body of works that contained the most radical and comprehensive social criticism ever formulated up to his time, a criticism whose impact on modern society was and remains incalculably great. Misunderstood and misrepresented by his contemporaries, he had written his *Confessions*—a unique act of self-exposure designed to prove to his detractors that even with all his weaknesses he was, like all men, fundamentally good. The posthumous publication of the *Confessions* only added to the misunderstanding and misrepresentation. Always his own worst enemy, and endowed with a sure instinct for making enemies of others, he saw to it that he would have a large number of them as long as people read books: the *Confessions* alone have supplied his detractors with virtually the entire arsenal of weapons they needed to attack him.

Rousseau was the victim not only of his enemies and of his mania for self-exposure, but also of his most enthusiastic followers. Indeed, like his critics, the majority of his admirers have obstinately persisted, down to our own times, in distorting his thought. They took from his writings only what they pleased, either to propagate or to attack what they chose to regard as his doctrine. He has been both claimed and damned by Marxists and conservatives, by atheists and mystics, by anarchists and totalitarians. He has been blamed with some plausibility for such disparate developments as the Reign of Terror, Hitlerism, progressive education, romantic love, liberalism, communism, nudism, momism, and the revival of square dancing. Everybody has read something about him, everybody thinks he knows what Rousseau said and preached; yet hardly anybody, whether admirer or enemy, seems to have taken the trouble to read him as attentively as he deserves. As a result, he has been almost universally credited with ideas that he either did not hold or that he held in common with most of his contemporaries, whereas the gist of his thought remains misunderstood. Before attempting to formulate what Rousseau did think, it is essential to dispose of at least five stereotyped falsehoods about him.

Falsehood 1: Rousseau preached a "return to nature." It is true that Rousseau, like Hobbes, assumed that man had lived in a state of nature before living in the state of society. Yet he insisted in his *Discourse on the Origin of Inequality*

that this hypothetical state of nature may never have existed and probably will never exist; he merely used it as a critical tool, or yardstick. He did not ask man to *return* to nature but simply to *turn* to her, and he expressly defended himself against the imputation that he wished man to turn back on the road he had already traveled. "Human nature does not retrogress," he wrote toward the end of his life; and, referring to himself in the third person, he continued: "He has been obstinately accused of wishing to destroy the sciences and the arts . . . and to plunge humanity back into its original barbarism. Quite the contrary: he always insisted on the preservation of existing institutions, maintaining that their destruction would leave the vices in existence and remove only the means to their cure."

Falsehood 2: Rousseau extolled primitive man, the "noble savage." The idea of the savage's moral superiority over the civilized European can be traced at least as far back as Montaigne, who wrote two centuries before Rousseau. The phrase "noble savage" occurs in Dryden; Rousseau never used it. American Indians and South Sea Islanders were extolled by Diderot and his collaborator Abbé Raynal, but not by Rousseau, who looked to Sparta, republican Rome, and his own native Geneva rather than to primitive societies. There is not a single exotic note in all his writings.

Falsehood 3: Rousseau began the cult of sensibility. He did not begin it; it was in full swing when he appeared on the scene, and though he contributed to its spread, so did the novelists Richardson and Sterne and the philosophers Shaftesbury and Diderot. The morbid sentimentality of the late eighteenth century—the fashionable fainting fits, floods of tears, suicides, romantic landscaping, and artificial rusticity—cannot be imputed to Rousseau, even though those who indulged themselves in these fads claimed him as their patron saint. Artificiality was precisely what he wished to eliminate from men's lives, and the antics of his misguided followers filled him with misgivings and scorn.

Falsehood 4: Rousseau reacted against the rationalism of his time and substituted feeling for reason as man's guide. This cliché contains two falsehoods. Far from being rationalist, the entire Enlightenment was a rebellion against Cartesian rationalism, metaphysics, and system making. It was an age of experimental science and empiricism, with Bacon, Locke, and Newton its guiding spirits. Voltaire, Diderot, and Hume no more rejected feeling than Rousseau rejected reason; what Rousseau did reject was intellectualism and the arrogance that goes with it. In assigning a primary place to feeling, conscience, or instinct, Rousseau was in complete harmony with his times.

Falsehood 5: Rousseau was the spiritual ancestor of the French Revolution. The early leaders of the Revolution looked more to Thomas Jefferson and the American Declaration of Independence than to Rousseau. Leaders of the later stages, such as Marat, Hébert, and Danton, were indifferent or hostile to Rousseau. Mme Roland and Robespierre, it is true, were fanatic Rousseauans—and two more opposed po-

Rousseau was painted in his "Armenian" costume by Allan Ramsay in 1766

litical thinkers it is difficult to imagine. All that can be said is that many revolutionists invoked Rousseau's name, and that Robespierre made the mad attempt to put his own version of Rousseau's political theory into practice; he emphasized the totalitarian features of Rousseau's *Social Contract* at the expense of its very spirit. The *Social Contract* is a theoretical blueprint for a society of equals; how such a society should come into existence Rousseau did not say, but it is quite plain that he never advocated the violent overthrow of existing institutions. Such was his respect for the customs and traditions of nations, such his aversion to forcing social change by mere legislation, that when he was asked by Polish liberals to propose a new constitution for Poland, his suggestions did not even provide for the immediate abolition of serfdom.

Every idea, every book, every act, has two sets of consequences—those intended and those not intended. It has just been shown that in at least five instances Rousseau is credited with an influence that he did not intend or that can be just as readily credited to others. Indeed, it may perhaps be said that no man since Christ has had more follies committed in his name. But it cannot be said that his *real* thought, the thought that was original with him, was of less consequence than were the ideas falsely imputed to him. Contemplating him from the vantage point of our own time, we see the gigantic and tortured figure of the prophet of modern man's predicament. Weak, sick in body and mind, perverted, unfit for society, he knew all the distress of the human condition, and he said, in essence: all man's sufferings are brought on him by man, not by God, who has given man the means to save himself.

"Everything is good as it leaves the hands of the Creator; everything degenerates in the hands of man"—the celebrated opening sentence of *Emile* contains all of Rousseau's thought in germ. All the conclusions he reached, no matter how mutually incompatible they may seem, can be traced to the same point of departure. And yet, for all the inner consistency of Rousseau's thought, it does not form a system; rather, it represents the application of the same emotional conviction to various fields. It is the intensely personal, subjective tone of his writings that lends them their force and that sparked the enthusiastic response they received. Regarding himself as both unique and universally human, Rousseau drew all his ideas from subjective experience. To understand what he thought, we must feel what he felt— hence the continuing emotional character of our reactions for or against him. It was the misery of his neuroses as much as the brilliance of his genius that made him the prophet of man's discontent with modern civilization. If we share his malaise (and who does not?), we should at least listen to him, though we do not have to agree with him.

Rousseau's birth, which took place in Geneva in 1712, cost his mother's life. His father, a watchmaker with a taste for travel, gave him an odd early education: he kept the boy up nights reading novels while he wept over the loss of

his wife. Rousseau's elder brother ran away to Germany as a boy and was never heard of again. When Jean Jacques was ten, his father had to leave Geneva as the result of some fracas. All in all, not a very settled family. Shortly after his father's flight, the boy experienced his first sexual pleasure while being spanked by the sister of the pastor with whom he was boarding. The perverse desire to repeat that experience remained with him all his life—although, as he asserts, he was too shy ever to ask from a woman the thing he desired most. Apprenticed to a watch engraver, he ran away at sixteen; became a Catholic convert (in return for a cash bonus) in Turin, where he served for a while as a lackey in a noble household; wandered off to Savoy, and there, in Chambéry or its environs, spent several years as the protégé,

*T*he world, Emile was told by the Savoyard Vicar, "is governed by a wise and powerful will." Such sentimental deism annoyed both the philosophes *and the Church: in 1762 Rousseau's* Emile *was condemned in Paris and Geneva.*

helpmate, adoptive son, and bedmate of a strange and remarkable woman, Mme de Warens, whom he called *Maman*.

Promiscuous in a motherly and dispassionate way, Mme de Warens was at the same time a devout Catholic in her own fashion, unbelievably kindhearted, and unbelievably irresponsible. She did not succeed in making Rousseau into a great lover, but she profoundly influenced his religious thought. Also, in the rustic idyll that he shared with her, Jean Jacques experienced—as he was to recall a few weeks before his death—the only period in his life when he felt entirely himself, the only time of which he could say that he had truly lived. *Maman*'s growing financial difficulties eventually forced him back into the world. We find him in Geneva, returning to the Protestant faith in order to regain his citizenship; we find him at Lausanne, giving piano lessons to young girls without himself being able to read a note of music (he was later to become a thoroughly competent musician); we find him wandering about Switzerland with a bogus archimandrite from Jerusalem, making speeches to raise funds; we find him in Paris, trying to make a fortune with a new system of musical notation he had invented. Everywhere his attractive looks, his obvious gifts, and the impression he conveyed of being made for better things, earned him the personal interest and patronage of those he met—among them some very eminent people. It was largely with their help and encouragement that he educated himself in the course of his wanderings. None of his writings betrays a lack of formal schooling.

His musical notation scheme was a fiasco, but he eventually obtained the post of private secretary to the French ambassador in Venice, where he gained an insight into the seamier sides of practical politics, had several bizarre and inconclusive love affairs, and, above all, gorged himself with music. The ambassador was an eccentric if not a maniac; after a while a resounding quarrel between the two men ended Rousseau's diplomatic career.

*B*ack in Paris and now in his thirties, Rousseau still had accomplished nothing, yet the happier half of his life was behind him. He fell in with the circle that soon was to acquire universal fame as the *philosophes* and *encyclopédistes* —Diderot and d'Alembert at their head, the publicist Frédéric-Melchior Grimm, and Grimm's mistress Mme d'Epinay. He also acquired a companion, Thérèse Levasseur, who worked as a servant girl at his lodgings and who was to remain by his side throughout the rest of his stormy and tragic career. In the winter of 1746–47, Thérèse bore him the first of five children, all of whom, according to his own testimony, he deposited at a foundling home, never to see them again. "In letting them become working people and peasants rather than adventurers and fortune hunters, I believed that I was acting as a good citizen and father," he explained later, without much conviction—though he may well have been right in his own case. Some have questioned whether Thérèse's children were really his; but even though Rousseau's sexual passion, extraordinarily intense as it was, remained largely confined to his imagination and to daydreams, there is no indication that he was impotent; or rather, he was impotent only with women whom he desired and loved passionately—and Thérèse was not one of them. It is certain that with his meager savings and his sporadic earnings as a literary hack and a music copyist he was scarcely in a position to support a family.

It was on a summer day in 1749, when he was entering his thirty-eighth year, that chance drove him into the career which was to make him both famous and wretched. He was walking to Vincennes to visit his friend Diderot, who was briefly and very comfortably imprisoned there. As he walked, he glanced at an announcement in a literary journal he was carrying, and read that the Academy of Dijon had proposed the following subject for its annual prize competition: Whether the restoration of the arts and the sciences has contributed to the purification of morals.

"If anything ever resembled a sudden inspiration," Rousseau wrote several years later in a letter, "it was the emotion that worked in me as I read that. I felt my spirit dazzled by a thousand lights; swarms of lively ideas presented themselves to me at once, with a force and confusion that threw me into an inexplicable turmoil; I felt my head seized with a dizziness like that of inebriation. A violent palpitation oppressed me and made my chest heave. Since I could no longer breathe while walking, I let myself drop under one of the trees by the wayside, and there I spent half an hour in such excitement that as I rose I noticed that the whole front of my jacket was wet with my own tears which I had shed without noticing it. Oh, Sir, If I could ever have written one fourth of what I had seen and felt under that tree, with what clarity I should have revealed all the contradictions of the social system! With what force I should have exposed all the abuses of our institutions! With what ease I should have shown that man is naturally good, and that it is through these institutions alone that men become bad. All I have been able to retain of these swarms of great truths that enlightened me in a quarter of an hour under that tree has been scattered quite feebly in my three main works."

Diderot afterward claimed that it was he who advised Rousseau to answer the academy's question in the negative and thus launched him on his career. Perhaps so; Rousseau later blamed Diderot for having made him insert extreme views in his *Discourse on the Sciences and the Arts* as well as in his *Discourse on Inequality*—views that indeed do not reappear in his later writings. It seems strange that the man who was just then editing the epoch-making *Encyclopedia, or Dictionary of the Sciences and the Arts,* should give such advice; but then Diderot probably felt that his friend had a better chance of winning the prize if he took the more original view, and besides he must have known that a negative answer would be more congenial to Rousseau's *farouche* temperament. At any rate, Rousseau's own account of his epiphany under the tree sounds completely convincing, and to imagine him answering the question as easily in the affirmative as in the negative is rather difficult.

Though overrhetorical, intemperate, and slightly confused, Rousseau's *Discourse* is so passionate and incandescent an indictment of civilization and material progress that even after two centuries it cannot leave the reader indifferent. In some respects the indictment was nothing novel: it echoes Thucydides, Cicero, Tacitus, and Plutarch, all of whom denounced the debilitating effects that luxury and ease produced on the moral fiber of society; yet, at the time when Rousseau's *Discourse* appeared, the more commonly held view was that the civilizing effect of higher living standards, industrial progress, luxury, and art would also produce a beneficent influence on man's moral conduct. To Rousseau, things looked different. Paris, that apex of civilization, appeared to him like a vast and nightmarish agglomeration of some five hundred thousand people who had come there to sell or prostitute their minds or bodies, to exploit others if they could, to impress each other with their wealth, their rank, their power, or their wits; half a million people busily scurrying about either to produce superfluous goods and services for their exploiters or doing nothing with an air of busy importance; polite to each other when expedient, but ready for treachery and caring only for themselves; alienated from the sources of true happiness; wretched in their hunt for success; stripped of the proud dignity of active citizens; thinking, acting, and striving not according to their own conscience and nature but according to the artificial standards of society. "No one," he wrote toward the end of his life, "cares for reality; everyone stakes his essence on illusion. Slaves and dupes of their self-love, men live not in order to live but to make others believe that they have lived."

Rousseau's *Discourse on the Sciences and the Arts* won the first prize it deserved. Though launched on a literary career and famous virtually overnight, he never renounced what he thought was his real vocation: he continued to write about music and even composed it. His opera *Le Devin du village,* a slight but charming work, was successfully performed before the King in 1752. Yet, half against his will, his newly gained reputation drew him into philosophy. He was accused of attacking the arts and sciences and of wanting men to go back to walking on all fours. The accusation, though unfair, forced him to explain himself and to clarify his position. If the arts and the sciences had failed to make men happier or more virtuous, the fault was not theirs but must be sought in the social institutions which perverted their ends. In his discourses *On the Origin of Inequality* and *On Political Economy* Rousseau's thought takes on a sharper focus: social institutions, almost everywhere and at all times, rest not on true law but on power; laws and conventions aim to consolidate the wealth and power of the *haves* and to reduce the *have-nots* to increasing dependency. Under the existing social institutions men had renounced the freedom of the state of nature without gaining the advantages of associating as equals for the common good. The law of the jungle still prevailed, but the innocence of animals was lost: "Thinking man is a depraved animal."

How man could raise himself above this wretched state is the theme of the two great works of Rousseau's maturity —*The Social Contract* and *Emile.* Perhaps Rousseau found the key to his quest in his epistolary exchange with Voltaire concerning the latter's poem on the Lisbon earthquake of 1755. Shocked by that terrible disaster, Voltaire questioned the existence of a benevolent God or Providence: God is said to be free, just, and clement. Then why, asks Voltaire, do we suffer so much under so mild a master? In reply, Rousseau pointed out that if people did not insist on gathering in large cities and on dwelling in six-story stone buildings, disasters on the scale of the Lisbon earthquake would be statistically less likely to occur. He went further: disbelief in God, or the possibility of a cruel or unjust God, was utterly unacceptable to him. "All the subtleties of metaphysics would not lead me to doubt for a moment the immortality of my soul or a spiritual Providence. I feel it, I believe it, I

As President of the revolutionist Convention, Robespierre staged a festival on June 8, 1794, honoring a Supreme Being to whom, by decree, he had just given official recognition. In Thomas Naudet's painting (above) the god dominates the fête from his elevated place near a Tree of Liberty; Wisdom sits on a pedestal at lower right;

desire it, and I will defend it to my last breath." And again: "In this strange contrast between what you prove and what I feel, I beg you to relieve my anxiety and to tell me where the deception lies—whether on the side of feeling or of reason." (Voltaire's reply was *Candide,* which Rousseau never read and which in fact leaves the question unanswered.)

In the words just quoted lies the key to Rousseau's religious and moral philosophy as he developed it in *Emile* and in his novel *Julie, or The New Héloïse,* and to which he gave expression most movingly and succinctly in the section of *Emile* entitled "The Profession of Faith of the Savoyard Vicar" (see page 96). Philosophy and theology, he contends, in all the thousands of years of their existence, have led us nowhere. We cannot be certain of anything except what we feel. Judgment and reasoning can enter only into our correlation of what we perceive through our senses.

and, standing on the steps leading to divinity, Robespierre harangues the crowd. Robespierre intended to impress upon France his own misguided interpretation of the deism in Rousseau's Social Contract—not the only time Rousseau has been made to play spiritual guest of honor at a celebration of ideas for which he had no sympathy.

Yet while we can never be wrong in feeling what we feel, we certainly can reason erroneously in relating our sense perceptions to one another. Reason and feeling must never be in conflict, but since reason is subject to error, it must always be controlled by feeling. The paradox disappears if one realizes that by "feeling," in this context, Rousseau always means "conscience."

To Rousseau, the purposes of God were unfathomable, as they are to most of us, and he derided as empty metaphysics any attempt to explain them. The hypothesis that the universe was the purposeful creation of a Supreme Being seemed to him incontrovertible simply because he *felt* it to be true, and who could convince him that he did not feel what he felt? Why there were seeming imperfections in the Creation he did not presume to say; like Alexander Pope, he felt that "in erring reason's spite/One truth is clear,

Whatever is, is right." And yet—this is the second great paradox in Rousseau's thought—it was plain that everything was wrong. "Everything is good as it leaves the hands of the Creator; everything degenerates in the hands of man" and the opening sentence of *The Social Contract*, "Man is born free, and everywhere he is in chains," are but two formulations of the same thought. What had gone wrong? Rousseau did not share the conviction of Voltaire's Dr. Pangloss that all was for the best in the best of all possible worlds; nor did his feeling allow him to accept the fashionable despair of later romantics and existentialists; nor did he find it possible to ascribe the sad state of our affairs to the Fall of Adam and Eve. To suppose that God would be so unreasonable and, one might say, inhuman as to create man simply in order to punish him for acting human went counter to reason and feeling. By endowing man with reason and with conscience, God had equipped him, in Rousseau's view, with everything he needed to pull himself up by his own bootstraps. Then why did everything degenerate in the hands of man? In answering the question, Rousseau substitutes for the Devil and Original Sin a new hypothesis: man is born good, but society corrupts him.

When we say nowadays that society is responsible for many of the crimes and sufferings in the world, we usually are unconscious of being Rousseauans; yet this idea, now a cliché, did originate with Rousseau, and in fact it is the weakest part of his philosophy. Rousseau's apparent inconsistency is twofold: (1) If man is good, then why does he become evil through association with other men, who are also good? (2) If society is the villain, then why does Rousseau prescribe the social contract as man's sole salvation? The questions would be well taken if it could be shown that Rousseau said society must necessarily corrupt man. But he never says such a thing. On the contrary, his entire social-contract theory is based on the assumption that the social state (not as it is, but as it might be) is a step forward from the state of nature. What is more, Rousseau maintained not only that just and beneficent societies were theoretically possible but that they had actually existed in the past—as in Sparta and republican Rome—and even in his own times, as in Geneva. (He soon was to revise that latter opinion.)

It is true nevertheless that, in Rousseau's opinion, society tends to corrupt man because it generally rests on power and exploitation rather than on law and co-operation. In a society not governed by law the individual moral will is stunted, social conventions take the place of inner conscience, men scramble after false values, self-love and vanity drown all benevolent instincts, and the gifts of life and nature pass unnoticed. All these evils are man-made and result from society, yet they are inherent neither in man nor in society. For man, it was Rousseau's conviction, is born not only with a conscience and with reason but also with a free will. He is the author of his fate, collectively speaking. Social redemption can be found in a collective exertion of the will by which men surrender all their individual rights to the body of society. Under such a "social contract," the state would be governed solely by the law, and the citizen could function at the same time as a free individual and as a member of a society whose exclusive goal is the common good. Indeed, "each man, by giving himself to all, gives himself to nobody"; and as long as no individuals or interest groups gain ascendancy over the rest, there will be a free and responsible citizenry. Thus, in the Rousseauan state, society cannot be answerable for the crimes and sufferings of individuals, nor can there be any leniency toward antisocial misfits.

Such are the basic features of Rousseau's *Social Contract*. That a theory of this sort should have been proposed by one of the most notorious social misfits in history must seem ironical, but it is not particularly surprising, nor does it invalidate its importance in modern political thought. But Rousseau was not content with abstract theory. A perfect society, he realized, would have to be a society of gods, and all human institutions carried the germs of their own decay within them. A good society could neither come into existence nor maintain itself for long unless its members had the necessary moral will. In *Emile*, which he wrote concurrently with *The Social Contract,* Rousseau attempted to show how man's inborn good instincts could be fostered and developed through education and how citizens worthy of the good society could be formed. Since existing society is corrupting, the pupil Emile is brought up far away from urban civilization by a tutor who serves as guide rather than teacher. No ready-made knowledge or moral code is imparted to him: all his learning is derived from direct experience, all his judgments spring from his own intellect and heart. While Rousseau failed in *Emile* to prove the innate goodness of man, he undoubtedly succeeded in laying the basis for modern pedagogy. All education since his day, whether progressive or traditional, rests to a large degree on Rousseau's psychological insights and moral goals.

The Social Contract deals with the good society, that is, a collective body; *Emile* deals with the good citizen, that is, the individual. Unlike some of his critics, Rousseau could see no contradiction between the two works. Within the collective state, the individual potentialities of its members could and should be developed in all their diversity, since free and rational men willing the common good could not help but agree on all essentials. While the two books complement rather than contradict each other, they nevertheless reveal the tension between two poles in Rousseau's temperament. Rousseau the champion of civic virtue and activity was also Rousseau the contemplative, solitary dreamer; a forerunner of Marxist collectivism, he was also one of the ancestors of romantic individualism and of Thoreau's civil disobedience. In both roles—the dour patriot and the eternal adolescent who plays hookey from class—Rousseau reacted against his social environment. This soon became apparent to his friends the *philosophes*, who tried to enlist him in their cause only to discover that he was not one of them.

Although, like him, they criticized society, society was the very air they breathed, whereas he revealed himself increasingly as a crank who shunned society and took offense at everything. The parting of the ways was gradual, but thanks to Rousseau's hypersensitive and morbidly suspicious nature, and to his radical alienation from society, it eventually became complete. "[He] makes me uneasy," Diderot wrote of their final meeting, "and I feel as if a damned soul stood beside me. . . . I never want to see that man again. He could make me believe in devils and in Hell."

The years Rousseau spent at the *Ermitage* and at Montmorency as the guest of Mme d'Epinay and, after breaking with her, as the guest of the Maréchal de Luxembourg were a period of growing isolation. To his friends, Rousseau was guilty of misanthropy, the worst crime in their eyes. To him, their devious methods to regain him for their fold appeared as persecution. At the same time he fell passionately in love with a much younger woman, the beautiful Mme d'Houdetot; since she was in love with another man, she did not reciprocate the middle-aged philosopher's ardor, and even if she had, she would have been disappointed, for, as Rousseau confesses, his passion was invariably spent in anticipation of their trysts. The ludicrous affair further envenomed Rousseau's relations with his meddling friends and undoubtedly helped to unhinge his mind. Yet it also produced a positive result. Jean Jacques, who was addicted to daydreaming and to populating (as he put it) the world with imaginary creatures, dreamed not only of ideal societies and ideal citizens but also of the ideal woman. He incorporated many of Mme d'Houdetot's features in her, called her Julie, and made her the heroine of his epistolary novel *Julie, or the New Héloïse.* With its sensuous descriptions of nature, its vibrant evocation of passion at its paroxysm, and its almost hysterical sensibility the book began a new era in literature, for better or for worse. At the same time its purpose is moral and its tone often quite preachy. Here the theme is the same as in *Emile* and *The Social Contract*: passions, pure in themselves, may overwhelm people whom society has not spoiled, but they can be transcended by the moral will.

By May of 1762 Rousseau had produced, within the space of two years, three of the most influential works of modern times. His later writings added nothing new and were intended only to justify himself before his fellow men. Indeed, the publication of *Emile* brought catastrophe upon him. It was, in particular, his merciless attack on revealed religion and on the authority of the Church (in the "Profession of Faith of the Savoyard Vicar") that drew him the simultaneous anathema of the Catholic Sorbonne in Paris and the Calvinist Consistory in Geneva. In both places warrants of arrest were issued against the author; in Paris, *Emile* was burned by order of Parliament, and as far away as the Netherlands and Switzerland it was officially condemned.

With the connivance of some very high-placed protectors, Rousseau escaped to Switzerland, finally settling at Motiers in what was then the Prussian principality of Neuchâtel. Though the works that had been condemned were reprinted in innumerable pirated editions, Rousseau saw in his fame only a new cause for persecution. The authorities denounced him as a godless rebel and a destroyer of society; his former friends, the *philosophes,* while ostensibly deploring the attacks on him, privately denounced him as a monster of ingratitude, a hater of men, a savage. His eccentric ways and clothes and his reputation for godlessness drew upon him the hatred of the local population; when he was stoned by a mob, he left Motiers and took refuge on the island of St. Pierre, in the Lake of Bienne, in Bernese territory. Two months later the government of Berne expelled him, although he had engaged in no more subversive activities than botanizing and boating. He accepted David Hume's invitation to join him in England. But his stay at Hume's country seat, at Wootton, ended with another resounding quarrel. In the eyes of the *philosophes* his blackness was demonstrated; they called him a tiger, and open war was declared.

Thus far, it would seem unfair to accuse Rousseau of persecution mania. His persecution had been very real. It is true that his isolation was due more to shyness and his exaggerated sensibility than to any initial hostility on the part of his friends, who at worst did not understand his neurotic personality. Even his persecution by the authorities can be largely ascribed to himself; the authorities had bent over backward to help him escape the consequences of measures they themselves had been forced to take because Rousseau insisted (unlike most of his contemporaries) on signing his most subversive writings with his real name. But that he was persecuted, that his friends had turned hostile and occasionally even vindictive, there can be no doubt. After his quarrel with Hume, however, his self-isolation and suspiciousness took on all the symptoms of paranoia.

Returning to France, where he was tolerated on condition that he refrain from publishing his writings, he wandered from place to place with his inseparable Thérèse, and finally fixed himself in Paris, living in poverty on his wages as music copyist, refusing to see anybody for long periods, brooding over his persecution. Everything that had happened to him in the past twenty-five years now appeared to him quite clearly as a universal plot for his destruction. His friends had secretly laid their traps years ago, while he was still unsuspecting; even those who had remained loyal were now suddenly revealing themselves as diabolical accomplices of the archplotter, Grimm. Occasionally he would try to defend himself against their slander by posting public notices, or would denounce their machinations in readings of parts of his *Confessions.* The second part of the *Confessions* reveals these paranoiac traits only too painfully; the dialogues entitled *Rousseau As Judge of Jean Jacques,* despite some brilliant flashes of reason, are even more tragic testimony to the growing darkness in his mind. Yet it would be bold to assert that Rousseau was demented. His last works, soliloquies really—the *Reveries of a Solitary Wan-*

derer—show by their serenity what a heroic victory he had gained over himself. He still believed in a universal plot against him, but reminding himself of the guiding principles of his own philosophy and of his capacity to find happiness in mere existence, he transcended his mania and found long periods of inner peace. "I laugh at the plots hatched by men," he declared, "and I enjoy my own being in spite of them." He died soon after writing these lines, at Ermenonville, north of Paris, where he was staying as the guest of one of his protectors.

Rousseau's *Confessions* probably remain his most widely read work. They are a unique, amazing, fascinating, shocking, moving, exasperating document. They have done more harm to the appreciation of Rousseau's thought than all the weaknesses that may be found in his other works put together. To psychiatrists, the document is perhaps as interesting for what its author reveals as for what—despite his genuine effort to say everything—remains concealed. It

Though Rousseau repudiated the idea, many who believed in the "noble savage" drew on his writings to support their belief—producing such idyllic visions as shown in the sketch above.

is only natural and fitting that students of the human soul should look at the *Confessions* with a clinical eye and regard the rest of his writings as the outpourings of a psychological cripple. It would be futile to deny that his attack on society was the result of resentment and social inadequacy, or that his compulsion to re-create the world in his imagination was induced by his inability to function "normally," by his sexual inhibitions and his autoerotic tendencies. Rousseau's personality was what psychologists would call immature; moreover, he suffered from a number of psychosomatic problems in addition to his psychological ones. Thus, while he was the reluctant lover of the motherly Madame de Warens, who regarded the act of love as a matter of male hygiene, Jean Jacques suddenly contracted some unusual and alarming symptoms which, according to him, lasted with undiminished intensity throughout the rest of his life; they involved a constant throbbing of his arteries accompanied by a loud noise in his ears in four different pitches. He also suffered from a malformation of the urethra, which caused urine retention. It was this condition that once made him refuse Louis XV's invitation to the Court and thus miss a chance of obtaining a royal pension. He was afraid of wetting himself in His Most Christian Majesty's presence, but he made his refusal appear the proud gesture of a citizen of a republic. The same weakness made him adopt, later on, what he called an Armenian costume—a caftanlike garment that was more comfortable than breeches but that seemed un-Christian to the inhabitants of Motiers.

Undoubtedly Rousseau's physiological and psychological handicaps go a long way toward explaining his reaction to society, yet such clinical discussions utterly fail to explain his influence or to invalidate his diagnosis of our social ills. It will never do to brush aside *The Social Contract* because its author lost his mother at birth or suffered from enuresis as a grown man. Oddly enough, however, such criticism is standard. Not only is it irrelevant, it also misrepresents Rousseau's personality.

*F*ar from being the antisocial recluse that he became after his contact with the world of fashion, finance, and intellect, Jean Jacques as a young man had been an exceptionally amiable and good-natured tramp. His penchant for vagrancy never left him. He loved to travel on foot, and he did not always end up at his intended destination. Though he did not shun work, he disliked working more than was necessary for his subsistence, and he treasured idleness above all things. The son of a watchmaker, he looked upon the day he threw away his watch as the beginning of his wisdom. He was fundamentally companionable, at least for the first five decades of his life. He was by no means prudish and, while no Casanova himself, was never a puritan censor of other people's sexual mores. Lacking the drives and ambitions of more settled and responsible men, he found his chief pleasure in the enjoyment of existence for its own sake, in daydreaming, in strolling through the countryside with his dog, in lying down under a tree. Until he experienced his famous illumination on the road to Vincennes, he was, unlike Saint Paul, the most harmless fellow in the world. Surely his sudden change from amiable vagabond to social and moral prophet must have had more immediate causes than a urethral obstruction.

The most obvious explanation is that the social evils which Rousseau diagnosed after his clash with Paris do in fact exist. While more robust temperaments could adjust to them, partly submitting to the inevitable, partly seeking a remedy in practical action ("Let us cultivate our garden," says Candide), Rousseau was by his nature compelled to challenge the entire system. Whether this was practical or wise is a matter for argument; it was inevitable and necessary, and it enabled him to penetrate to the very roots of modern man's dilemma. Science and material progress had not made men happy. On the contrary, in their pursuit of false values, men had forgotten to learn from nature.

*J*eaurat de Bertry's crowded Allegory of the Revolution *pictures Rousseau as the Revolution's spiritual father. Rousseau presides over a jumble of symbols that include a monument to Equality (at left), two maidens representing Goodness and Good Faith, a bundle of rods and war axes (efficient administration, with the ability to enforce laws) topped by the red Cap of Liberty, the Eye of Providence emitting the light of Wisdom, a Tree of Liberty, unfinished columns (the bases of regeneration), a soldier of the Revolution, and, in the dim background, a guillotine.*

Rather than be themselves, they strove for the creation of a desirable image of themselves in the eyes of their fellow men. Governed by the opinions of others, they had ceased to be individuals without becoming members of a community. Sacrificing their birthright as citizens and self-determined beings for the sake of security, pleasure, and comfort, they invited the destruction of all freedom. Born free and with the gift of reason, they lived as slaves and dupes. These causes of unhappiness could be blamed neither on God nor on human nature: far from commanding man to submit to fate, God or nature had endowed him with the means to shape his fate. Nature, to Rousseau, did not appear cruel—only natural. But man had become perverse since he used his natural gifts to impress and oppress other men instead of living with them in a free and brotherly community.

Whether one agrees or disagrees with Rousseau's prescriptions, it is impossible not to recognize that his persistent theme, that man's alienation from nature is the price of modern civilization, continues to vex us. His insistence that only man can save himself, that the tools are not lacking but only the will, is truer in our technological age than it was in his own. It is because of this that Rousseau was a prophet. How to simplify man's existence in an increasingly complicated culture remains the great problem. If man is not born good, as Rousseau thought he was, at least he is born with the potentiality for good; and he has reached the point where, if he does not realize that potentiality by a collective effort of the will, he must perish.

J. Christopher Herold, a frequent contributor to HORIZON, *wrote "Our Great Favourite, Miss Austen" for the Spring, 1964, issue.*

For further reading: Jean-Jacques Rousseau: A Critical Study of His Life and Writings *by F. C. Green (Cambridge University Press, 1955);* Protestant Thought: From Rousseau to Ritschl *by Karl Barth (Harper & Brothers, 1959);* The Question of Jean-Jacques Rousseau *by Ernst Cassirer, translated by Peter Gay (Indiana University Press, 1963);* Jean-Jacques Rousseau: A Study in Self-Awareness *by Ronald Grimsley (Dufour, 1962);* The Party of Humanity *by Peter Gay (Knopf, 1964).*

UPMANNSHIP

The Cigar smoker is an amiable, well-balanced sort of fellow, generally to be found in deep leather armchairs where he passes his time thinking long thoughts and tugging contemplatively at the ears of Irish setters. These are our normal attitudes and postures. We are a worthy group, more to be encouraged than harassed. Yet it is we, of all people, who have suffered over the past few years a series of shocks that have made our present harrowing, and our future dubious. It is too much.

First came the events that cut us off abruptly from our source of Cigars, all because of what *Pravda* has tellingly described as "the well-known bankruptcy of American foreign policy." Let the defenders of this policy say what they will, we Cigar smokers look upon the events of October, 1962, as the Cuban Cigar Crisis, and we know it as a defeat. The missiles, it is true, were cleared from Cuban soil, but the Cigars were permitted to remain.

(It might be advisable, at this point, to state the distinction between Cigars and cigars, just as one must occasionally point out to a Californian the distinction between Burgundy and burgundy. To obtain a Cigar, one persuades a man in Cuba to grow tobacco, and other men in Cuba to dry it, cure it, age it, and roll it into long cylinders which are then themselves wrapped in tobacco. In no other manner may a Cigar be manufactured. A cigar, on the other hand, may differ from a Cigar merely in that the last stage of its manufacture takes place in Tampa, Florida; at the other extreme it is quite possible to create a cigar in Passaic, New Jersey, out of decayed vegetation. In either case the cigar is not, nor can it ever become, a Cigar.)

Staggering in disarray, we next found the Surgeon General telling the American public what we cigar smokers had known all along: that cigarettes were noxious, toxic, and malevolent. At once a horde of barbaric valetudinarians invaded our ranks. We were overrun by Goths and Vandals, each with a five-pack of Phillies Blunts (or the equivalent) tucked into his shirt pocket, and not an Irish setter in the lot.

We must now stand by and watch one of these Genghis Khans, lately terrified out of the cigarette habit, as he whips the cellophane from a sodden brown object with a wrapper of reconstituted tobacco leaf and a plexiglas tip, sets the roaring fire of a cigarette lighter to its end, puffs furiously for two minutes, and walks down the street with a flaming torch outthrust from his mouth. If it were a Cigar he was lighting, we would have him up for arson. As it is, it merely saddens us, as if we were Athenians watching a crap game in the Parthenon.

There is, of course, only one proper way to light a Cigar, or even an honorably made cigar. To begin with, one must be provided with a long sliver of wood, or "spill," which may be procured in London at a modest price, or which one can make for oneself by chopping down a tree, letting it dry for a year or two, and shaving off splinters from it. The process begins with the tip of the cigar held between the thumb and forefinger of the right hand; they press gently upon it until the tip breaks open and an air passage takes shape. The cigar is then transferred to the left hand and the spill taken in the right hand. The spill

By STEPHEN WHITE

is plunged into the fireplace and set alight. The end of the cigar is rotated in the flame of the spill until it is hot, whereupon the cigar is taken into the mouth, its end still in the flame. A slow, gentle draft of air is then drawn through the cigar, which lights evenly and coolly. The entire process can be carried out hastily in two minutes, or deliberately in five. No true Cigar smoker will light a Cigar in any other fashion. True, one's living room becomes hot in midsummer with a fire always burning in the fireplace, but we know where our pleasure lies, and we put up with minor discomforts.

The care taken in lighting a Cigar is the culmination of a long history of care. A Cigar, for example, must never be dry and must never be wet. Balance is everything, as in feeding liquor to a woman at a cocktail party: err in one direction and the party is ruined; err in the other and the woman is ruined. A humidity carefully maintained at around 70 per cent is about right, for both cigars and women. Incidentally this balance cannot be achieved, for cigars at least, by wrappings. A cigar that is wrapped in cellophane, or an aluminum tube, or any such frippery, is no longer a cigar. It is a dead leaf, and should be decently buried.

There is much more that can be said—about the shape of a cigar, the ritual that accompanies the selection of a cigar, and the manner in which expelled smoke is most efficiently directed upward toward the nostrils. It might be better, however, to comment upon the question now being asked on television: "Should a gentleman offer a Tiparillo to a lady?"—or more generally, *any* cigar. The answer is No. For one thing, there is the matter of cigar ash. The ash on a cigar plays a definite role in cigar smoking; by radiating heat from the end of the cigar, it helps keep the cigar cool (and it is vitally important that the cigar remain cool). For this reason, ash must never be tapped from a cigar. It must be ignored. Ultimately, of course, a long ash will topple of its own weight, falling on the smoker's vest. Ladies, for several reasons, all of which I applaud, do not wear vests and should not be encouraged to do so. Hence, by inexorable logic, they should not smoke cigars. There are other reasons as well, all of which may be summed up in the statement that by giving a cigar to a lady one reduces the likelihood of obtaining the maximum gratification from either.

All this is the lore of the cigar, and most of it bespeaks a way of life that is passing. But hope remains. It is an interesting peculiarity of cigar smoking that—in a useful phrase recently become current—it escalates. A smoker accustomed to a ten-cent cigar one day tries a fifteen-cent cigar, and thereafter can never go back. Instead he progresses, accident by accident, from fifteen cents to a quarter, from a quarter to three for a dollar, and then forward to fifty cents—ever onward and Upmann-ward. As the cigars get better, the meanest individual acquires a respect for them, until the day comes when he goes out searching for spills. Meanwhile lights burn late in Washington, and someday a shipment of Cigars will arrive again. Let us not mourn our past: let us look hopefully toward the future.

AT THE BALL

CULVER PICTURES

PICTORIAL PARADE

THE SUNDAY DRIVE

WIDE WORLD PHOTOS

THE BILLIONAIRE

CULVER PICTURES

PICTORIAL PARADE

THE GRAND LOBBY

THE GRAND LOBBY

IS
THIS
PROGRESS ?

Collected by Max Brandel

ROYAL ATTIRE

WIDE WORLD PHOTOS

WIDE WORLD PHOTOS

THE CROSSING

"THE INTIMATE OF EVERY HOUSEHOLD"

Thus was Charles Dickens described by The Times *on the day after he died, June 10, 1870. Here, nearly a hundred years later, an equally prolific English novelist appraises the lasting virtues of Dickens and his great English* Comédie humaine

By COMPTON MACKENZIE

This unfinished painting by a Victorian artist named Robert William Buss shows Charles Dickens in the study at Gad's Hill, his country home in Kent, surrounded by his literary offspring. Little Nell, his favorite, is perched on his knee; Paul Dombey appears just above his right hand, and Sam Weller in the upper left corner. All these characters throng the air as they have thronged the imaginations of generations of Dickens lovers. In this painting the artist copied some of the etchings of Dickens's most famous illustrator, Hablot K. Browne, known as "Phiz." Some details from Phiz etchings appear on the next six pages.

Coincidence ruled that the two novels in which Thackeray and Dickens allowed themselves to use the most autobiographical material were written within a year of one another. *David Copperfield* was the eighth full-length novel written by Charles Dickens; *Pendennis* was the third written by William Makepeace Thackeray.

It may be postulated that no major male novelist has had recourse to autobiography for his first novel. This is not to deny greatness to the subjective or, in the jargon of the moment, introverted novelists like the Brontës or Proust or Joyce or Lawrence. Blake was a greater poet than Tennyson, but he is a minor poet; Tennyson is a major poet. The primary aim of a minor novelist is to portray life and illuminate it through his own vision, and by the intensity of that vision he achieves greatness or remains insignificant. The primary aim of a major novelist is to tell a story and, in telling that story, to portray life as intelligibly as he can through various aspects of it to as many various readers as possible. If he can give authentic life to the characters in his tale, whether they be portraits or caricatures or creations of his own fancy, such a major novelist will achieve greatness; otherwise he will remain a mere writer of *feuilletons.* André Gide, himself a minor novelist, once called the *Comédie humaine* of Balzac a great fresco crumbling to pieces a little more all the time. If that be true, then the novel as an art form is on the way to extinction; it means that supreme masters of fictional narrative like Balzac, Scott, and Dickens are no longer capable of stirring the imagination of contemporary youth, and will be even more incomprehensible to a human future under the merciless sway of its own inventiveness—a future when man will have only his sexual experience to convince him that he is still an individual.

Charles Dickens was a perfervid individualist, and so there is irony in the fact that the reforms he so ardently desired to see could only have been carried out by Parliament with the help of the civil service, both of which he never lost an opportunity to mock. When, apropos of *Hard Times*—which is bitter propaganda on behalf of the working classes—Macaulay called Dickens a "sullen socialist," the complacent Whiggery of Macaulay was, as usual, wrong; Dickens would have been exasperated by a tenth of the socialism we have today.

Speaking as David Copperfield, Dickens allows his hero to reveal much of the character of his creator: "Whatever I have tried to do in life, I have tried with all my heart to do well . . . whatever I have devoted myself to, I have devoted myself to completely . . . in great aims and in small, I have always been thoroughly in earnest. I have never believed it possible that any natural or improved ability can claim immunity from the companionship of the steady, plain, hard-working qualities, and hope to gain its end."

And again Copperfield claims—speaking, one feels sure, for Dickens himself—that he never put one hand to anything on which he could not throw his whole self; and never affected depreciation of his work, whatever it was. Would that all popular authors could claim as much!

Charles Dickens was born in Portsmouth on February 7, 1812, and died on June 9, 1870. His childhood may be said to have been spent in the lingering eighteenth century, while in the year of his death, which saw the passing of the Forster Education Act, the twentieth century was dimly visible. He was the son of John Dickens, a clerk in the Navy Pay Office. In 1814 John

Mr. Pickwick and Sam Weller

Dickens was transferred to Somerset House and in 1817 to Chatham. Here Charles lived happily until he was ten years old, and for the rest of his life Kent was to be the county of his heart as London was to be the city of his mind.

Mrs. Dickens taught her little son to read and to write and was even able to give him some elementary Latin. After a time, the extravagant good fellowship of John Dickens, of whom traces are discernible in the immortal figure of Mr. Micawber, made it necessary for the family to move to a cheaper house in Chatham. Charles went to school when he was eight and was well taught for two years. More important than what he learned at school was his discovery of some odd volumes in an unused room— *Don Quixote, Tom Jones, Roderick Random, Peregrine Pickle, The Vicar of Wakefield, Robinson Crusoe,* and *The Arabian Nights.* Charles was a delicate child, often subject to spasms of pain. Therefore he did not indulge in sports with his school companions, but read these magic volumes instead. This boyhood reading has always had for me a profound appeal because I, too, a somewhat delicate and lonely child until I was seven years old, read those same volumes over and over again. I had, however, one

great advantage that Charles Dickens did not enjoy: I was able to read at the same time *Oliver Twist, Dombey and Son, The Pickwick Papers, Nicholas Nickleby,* and *Martin Chuzzlewit.* To this day, more than seventy years later, these remain by far my favorite novels by Dickens.

By 1822 matters were becoming financially difficult in Chatham and John Dickens moved his family to Camden Town, which at this date was a kind of experimental garden suburb. Many of Dickens's commentators, misled by the squalid reputation and appearance of the neighborhood for the last hundred and thirty years, have not realized that this squalor is due to the railways. In whatever part of London a railway terminus has been built, its inevitable effect has been to destroy the decency of its neighborhood.

The financial situation of John Dickens went from bad to worse. Mrs. Dickens tried to start a school in Gower Street, but it failed within months. In 1824 John Dickens was arrested for debt and sent to the Marshalsea prison. About this time, Charles was given the job of pasting labels in a shoe-blacking factory on the edge of the Thames. For this he was paid six shillings a week. Dickens never forgave this humiliation, but we can be glad he suffered it.

Mr. Mantalini

Without any doubt those months in the blacking factory were the making of him as the mighty novelist he was to become, coupled as they were with the family's res-

idence in the Marshalsea, the background of which was forever imprinted in Dickens's memory—that photographic memory which in the words of David Copperfield looked at nothing but saw everything.

By the end of that miserable year John Dickens had managed to pay off his creditors from a legacy, and the family moved to Somers Town, where Charles went to Mr. Jones's Classical and Commercial Academy in the Hampstead Road; here he was well taught by the standards of the time, and when he left the school at Easter in 1827, he was head boy. He was now fif-

Mr. Pecksniff

teen, and became first the office boy to a solicitor and a month or two later the clerk to a firm of lawyers in Gray's Inn. Then he learned shorthand and in 1829 became court reporter to the Court of Doctors' Commons, a post he held for about two years. (Doctors' Commons would be the Probate, Admiralty, and Divorce Court of today; British conservatism is always chary of excessive change—hence the absurdity of entrusting matrimonial affairs, wills, and nautical matters to the same Court.) This legal experience gave Dickens a professional interest in the machinery of the Law; one feels the relish with which he put into the mouth of Bumble the immortal remark, "If the law supposes that, the law is a ass— a idiot."

In 1831 Dickens was engaged as a parliamentary reporter for an evening paper for which he took down the speeches on the

Reform Bill, becoming as contemptuous of "the great dust heap of Westminster" as he already had become of the Law. No doubt Dickens himself would have been shocked if he had been called an anarchist, but fundamentally that is what he was. By the following year Dickens had established himself as the fastest and best reporter of parliamentary and political speeches in the country. And now, under the pseudonym of Boz, he began to write articles. Only twenty-one years of age, he had already taken a degree with first-class honors in the University of Life; he had also read assiduously in the British Museum to help a conventional education.

Sketches by Boz appeared anonymously at first, but soon Dickens realized the importance of a name, even if it were a pseudonym. Nowadays one always hears "Boz" pronounced as "Bozz"; in fact, it should be pronounced "Boze." Dickens had a younger brother nicknamed Moses, after Goldsmith's Moses in *The Vicar of Wakefield,* which became Boses during a heavy cold; shortened to Boz, it gave the elder brother the pseudonym he was to make famous. Harrison Ainsworth introduced Dickens to John Macrone, who published two volumes of *Sketches by Boz* in the week of Dickens's twenty-fourth birthday. They had a good sale. They attracted the attention of the newly established publishers Chapman and Hall, who offered Dickens fourteen pounds a month to write the adventures of a Nimrod club, "the members of which were to go out shooting, fishing and so forth, and getting themselves into difficulties through their want of dexterity." These adventures were to be published in monthly installments and were to provide the artist-cartoonist Robert Seymour with opportunities for illustrations. Dickens invented Nathaniel Winkle as the absurd sportsman, but pressed to be allowed to widen the scope of what later became the Pickwick Club. Dickens found Seymour impossible to work with, but after the first couple of numbers poor Seymour shot himself and a hurried search was made for a new illustrator. Thackeray, who started out as an artist,

was one of the applicants for the job that was eventually given to Phiz (Hablot K. Browne), whose illustrations for *Pickwick* and all the other novels that followed in the next twenty years will be forever inseparably associated with them by their readers.

Mark Tapley

It is easy to see that in the beginning Dickens was by no means happy about the task he had set himself, and for the first four months, April through July, 1836, *Pickwick Papers* was a failure. Then, in the fifth number, Sam Weller appeared, and by the time the serial was finished in November, 1837, the sales had risen from four hundred to forty thousand. At the age of twenty-five Charles Dickens had arrived to stay for a longer period of universal popularity than any novelist had ever achieved or is ever likely to achieve in the future. Five months after Queen Victoria ascended the throne in 1837, *Pickwick Papers* was published as a volume, by which time *Oliver Twist* was appearing monthly in *Bentley's Miscellany.* Dickens had written to Chapman and Hall, "If I were to live a hundred years, and write three novels in each, I should never be so proud of any of them, as I am of Pickwick."

Dickens was right to be proud of *Pickwick,* which displays his fecund genius at its richest and reveals little of its weaknesses. It is no exaggeration to assert that the sum total of comic figures created by novelists writing in English before Charles Dickens was surpassed in a single volume written by a young man before he was twenty-six years of age—and all these Dickens characters are alive today. Yet even as an octogenarian

makes that statement, he asks himself whether in fact it is true. He remembers that the eccentric figures of his youth had no difficulty in accepting the reality of the portraits, but he wonders whether they seem as real to the young reader of today.

"I saw *Hamlet: Prince of Denmark* played: but now the old plays began to disgust this refined age." That was an entry in John Evelyn's diary for 1661; those of us who feel like anachronisms today, as far as literary tastes are concerned, can always reassure ourselves by reflecting that once upon a time Shakespeare was out of fashion with the avant-garde.

Before *Oliver Twist* was finished, Dickens was already writing *Nicholas Nickleby,* which had an even more fantastic success than its predecessors.

In *Oliver Twist* Dickens had revealed his melodramatic skill; this was confirmed in *Nicholas Nickleby,* without detracting in the least from his comic invention. Mrs. Nickleby had a bit of Dickens's own mother

Mrs. Gamp

in her, but so little that Mrs. Dickens did not recognize herself. Nobody has suggested an original for Mr. Mantalini; he may have been a figment of Dickens's own exuberant imagination and genuine creative genius. An inspired novelist or dramatist like Dickens or Ibsen has no need of models for even his most vital characters, although inevitably, as these characters proliferate, he will be driven to use models from time to time.

"'I am ashamed of you,' said Madame Mantalini, with much indignation.

"'Ashamed? Of *me*, my joy? It knows it is talking demd charming sweetness, but naughty fibs,' returned Mr. Mantalini. 'It knows it is not ashamed of its own popolorum tibby.'"

In contrast to Mr. Mantalini, who went "to the demnition bow-wows," another rascal, Sir Mulberry Hawk, never comes to life. In his youth Dickens lacked opportunities to observe what used to be called Society, and even in his maturity—when he had every opportunity to mix with it—he never produced a real aristocrat.

Nicholas Nickleby was followed by *The Old Curiosity Shop.* It is difficult for us today to understand what an effect the death of Little Nell had upon people in Britain and America, not to mention the author himself. Even Carlyle blubbered over it; as for Dickens, he wrote to his friend John Forster: "Nobody will miss her like I shall. It is such a very painful thing to me, that I really cannot express my sorrow."

It has been suggested that in the nine-

Mr. Dombey

teenth century, when so many human beings were exploited in the interest of greed, sentimental emotion and religious ostentation served as sedatives for the conscience of the well-to-do. Dickens's outbursts against what he considered abuses made more conservative opinion suspect him of radicalism. Yet he remained untouched by

prison reform (apart from making a protest against public executions) or the iniquities of lunatic asylums.

Barnaby Rudge, set in the time of the

Carker

George Gordon anti-popery riots, was a great success when it appeared in weekly installments, but it is probably the least read of Dickens's novels today. Yet it contains one character who is worthy of attention—Simon Tappertit, the little man with big ideas about himself. Simon Tappertit is a more plausible figure today than he was when Dickens created him, and a much more potentially dangerous figure. The egalitarian trend of the time favors the herd, and when one of the herd, however little, becomes a rogue, he can do as much damage as an elephant. Simon Tappertits abound today on both sides of the Atlantic.

In June, 1841, Dickens visited Edinburgh to be received by that reputedly cold and phlegmatic city with the rapture we associate today with polygamous film stars or browless pop singers. He wrote to Forster that his hotel was literally besieged. "I have been forced to take refuge in a sequestered apartment at the end of a long passage."

At the end of the month he was given the freedom of the city; he was still seven months away from his thirtieth birthday! A note of exclamation is justified. No such recognition had ever been offered to an English author of any age, and it can safely be prophesied that no such recognition

will ever be offered in the future, at any rate to a novelist under thirty.

Dickens had for some time wanted to go to the United States, where his work had been as popular as it was in Great Britain. At the beginning of 1842 he set sail from Liverpool with his wife, Catherine Hogarth, to whom he had been married for just on six years. They arrived in Boston on January 21 and went on by way of Hartford to New York. At the dinners given in his honor Dickens was honest (or as some thought, tactless) enough to complain of the fact that there was no copyright for his books in America. Indeed, at that date international copyright did not exist. Not even Scott's books had enjoyed as great a circulation as those of Dickens, thousands upon thousands of which were sold in the United States without the author's receiving a penny. On the back of a volume of reminiscences by my great-grandfather, published in 1844 by Harper, *A Christmas Carol* is advertised at what seems the preposterous price of 3 1/4 cents. At the Boston dinner that lasted from five o'clock in the afternoon until one o'clock in the morning the books of Charles Dickens were lauded in speech after speech, but when the author suggested he should be rewarded with more than words, he was attacked by the American press for being mercenary.

The publication of *American Notes,* soon after Dickens returned to England, did not please the Americans, and indeed they are too facile and superficial. However, the resentment felt over *American Notes* was slight compared with the fury Dickens roused in 1843–44 with *Martin Chuzzlewit* and its picture of the United States drawn for a British public only too anxious at this date to hear the worst of Americans. The figures are all caricatures of the crudest kind, as lifeless as Dickens's ludicrous attempts to portray English aristocracy.

Yet he can very easily be forgiven for his failure to conjure up the American scene accurately—for without *Martin Chuzzlewit* we should not have the immortal figures of Mr. Pecksniff and Mrs. Gamp to delight us, not to mention lovable Mark Tapley and the humors of Todgers's, that London boardinghouse so much more familiar to Dickens than the Mississippi.

The mere mention of Mrs. Gamp tempts one to quote that disreputable old midwife as she used to quote her mysterious friend, Mrs. Harris. " 'Bother Mrs. Harris!' said Betsy Prig. . . . 'I don't believe there's no sich a person!' "

One of Mrs. Gamp's observations must suffice: "Some people may be Rooshans, and others may be Prooshans; they are

Solomon Gills

born so, and will please themselves. Them which is of other naturs think different."

That remark may be commended to the attention of political theorists in Great Britain and the United States today.

A Christmas Carol appeared at the end of 1843; it is hardly an exaggeration to say that it has become a fairy tale which we all believe must really once have happened— like Cinderella or Dick Whittington or Rip Van Winkle.

Dickens traveled much in France, Switzerland, and Italy during the next two years, but he was never able to grasp the European attitude to life. It is significant to find him writing from Lausanne in August, 1846, when he was beginning *Dombey and Son,* of how much he missed the London streets, especially at night. "I can't express how much I want these. It seems as if they supplied something to my brain, which it cannot bear, when busy, to lose."

When the first installment of *Dombey and*

Son appeared in October, 1846, its success was immediate and its sales exceeded those of *Martin Chuzzlewit* by more than twelve thousand copies. Dickens himself thought well of it. When it was published as a book in 1848, he wrote in a letter: "I have great faith in Dombey, and a strong faith that it will be remembered and read years hence." His faith was justified; it has probably been more widely read than any of Dickens's novels except *Pickwick* and *David Copperfield.* Thackeray wrote a letter of generous praise while *Dombey* was appearing serially at the same time as *Vanity Fair,* which in his grateful reply Dickens said he was saving up to read until *Dombey* was done.

Apart from the preposterous villain Carker, Dickens keeps a brake on melodrama in *Dombey and Son.* The death of Paul Dombey is moving, but avoids luscious sentimentality much more successfully than Dickens avoided it in the death of Little Nell. This is the first novel in which he recognizes the arrival of the railway; he uses the new mechanical monster to dispose of that almost equally mechanical monster, Carker. There is irony in the fact that nearly twenty years hence Dickens himself would be involved in one of those serious railway accidents whose frequency

Captain Cuttle

drew such a stern rebuke from Queen Victoria.

Immortal comic characters abound in *Dombey and Son.* There are Solomon Gills, the maker of nautical instruments, and his

friend Captain Cuttle with his one arm and his advice, "when found, make a note of." There is dear Susan Nipper, the devoted maid of Florence Dombey. "I may not be Methosalem, but I am not a child in arms." There is Major Bagstock, the archetype of

Major Bagstock

how many comic majors, not one of whom came to life as authentically as Major Joseph B. Bagstock himself, "one of the old Bagstock breed."

Dickens was almost thirty-seven years old when he set out to write what is generally allowed to be his greatest novel. *David Copperfield* was published in book form at the end of 1850 when he was close to thirty-nine. "Of all my books, I like this the best," he declared. Posterity has agreed with him. Thackeray's *Pendennis* was appearing as a serial at the same time. It is tempting to turn aside and talk of the relations between the two men, but it would add nothing to any literary judgment of their work. They were both friends of my grandfather. Contemporary opinion regarded Thackeray as a cynic, Dickens as a socialist. Both opinions seem equally absurd to us today.

Undoubtedly, Dickens was able to reveal more of his essential personality in the first fourteen chapters of *David Copperfield* than in anything else he wrote. That there was something of Dickens's father in Mr. Micawber is certain; there was also something of Dickens's mother in Mrs. Micawber. Although both are essentially the products of their creator's own rich fecundity, we may probably hear an echo of John Dickens in: "Annual income twenty pounds, annual expenditure nineteen nineteen six, result happiness. Annual income twenty pounds, annual expenditure twenty pounds ought and six, result misery."

Nobody has suggested an original for David's aunt, Betsy Trotwood; she is just the most vivid portrait in the long gallery of old maids painted by Dickens. It is Miss Trotwood who has taken charge of Mr. Dick, that endearing lunatic who "had been for upwards of ten years endeavouring to keep King Charles the First out of the Memorial [on his affairs] but he had been constantly getting into it, and was there now." That intrusion of King Charles's head has become proverbial in the English language. The memorable characters in *David Copperfield* seem inexhaustible. Who can ever forget Mrs. Gummidge's determined melancholy? "I am a lone lorn creetur', and everythink goes contrairy with me." Or Barkis the carrier? "When a man says he's willing, it's as much as to say,

David Copperfield

that man's awaitin' for a answer," the answer being to what he considered a proposal of marriage. "It was as true as taxes is," said Mr. Barkis on one occasion, "and nothing is truer than them." Or Miss Mowcher, another from Dickens's gallery of old maids? "What a world of gammon and spinnage it is, though, ain't it!" Or the villainous clerk, Uriah Heep? One could quote endlessly from that wonderful book. Admittedly, it could be cut in places; Dickens's method of publishing his novels

serially as he wrote them inevitably led to occasional padding.

Bleak House followed *David Copperfield.* This is a satire upon the old Court of Chancery which, although it annoyed the

Mr. Micawber

lawyers, led to reforms. Again we have a gallery of imaginary portraits painted with Dickens's prodigal hand. In *Bleak House* he did use two models—Harold Skimpole is a real portrait of Leigh Hunt, and Lawrence Boythorn of Walter Savage Landor. One may fancy that he hoped to smooth Leigh Hunt's ruffled feelings by bringing in another recognizable author, who, although presented more sympathetically, was almost as annoyed as Leigh Hunt.

Bleak House has some masterly London landscapes, but Dickens seems for the first time to be turning against the city he had already immortalized. In *Bleak House* London is an enemy; its fogs are sinister. Dickens essays a picture of county society without much success and with even less success tells some of the story through the medium of Esther Summerson's diary. Fortunately for his readers, he did not repeat this mistake: he was a good actor but he was not suited to play female ingénues, however well he might enact pantomime dames. Yet, what does Dickens's failure to portray Esther Summerson matter when we remember the pompous humbug Chadband; the cunning lawyer Tulkinghorn;

Turveydrop, that model of deportment; Guster, the poor slavey; Miss Flite, the little mad lady who haunts the Chancery Courts; Jo, the crossing sweeper, whom the police were ever chivying, to his death at last; and as many more characters?

Hard Times, which was serialized in *Household Words* during 1854, must be called a dull novel. Dickens wanted to write about industrial strife, but a hurried visit to Preston in Lancashire during a strike merely provided him with enough local color to daub on too obviously. On the other hand, in the next novel, *Little Dorrit,* the local color is the best part of it, for Dickens knew the Marshalsea in the days when his father was imprisoned there. *Little Dorrit* was an outstanding success when it was being serialized in 1856–57, but contemporary criticism was disinclined to respect the verdict of the general public. I have always found the book protracted, the subsidiary melodrama more than usually extravagant, and the satire on the Circumlocution Office heavy-handed. Yet, once again, no sooner has one criticized the flaws than one remembers the gems. No one can forget the advice of Mrs. General, the lady companion of old Dorrit's two daughters: "Father is rather vulgar, my dear. The word Papa, besides, gives a

Mr. Barkis

pretty form to the lips. Papa, potatoes, poultry, prunes, and prisms are all very good words for the lips . . ."

Dickens's next novel, *A Tale of Two*

Cities, was published as a book in 1859, after running serially in the new paper he had founded called *All the Year Round.* The presentation of the French Revolution

Miss Mowcher

was as conventional as almost every presentation of it in fiction has been since Carlyle wrote about it. There are moments of Dickens at his best, but also a faint suggestion that the most prolific creator of characters in the English language is beginning to get tired.

In the last ten years of his life Dickens produced only three novels; the last of them, *The Mystery of Edwin Drood,* he did not live to solve. *Great Expectations* had perhaps the best opening Dickens ever wrote, but the promise of the beginning is not sustained by the interest he is able to rouse in the development of his story. *Our Mutual Friend* was published in 1865 when Dickens was fifty-three. It revived from time to time memories of the master's touch when London seemed to belong to him. The riverside scenes are as good as any he ever painted; Mr. Podsnap and the Veneerings, as vivid and true as any characters.

Charles Dickens's total output as a novelist is impressive enough, but we have to remember that it was being achieved simultaneously with continuously astonishing displays of vitality, mental and physical alike, in the course of not much more than thirty years. He edited *Household Words* and *Master Humphrey's Clock,* and then at forty-seven, a time of life when so many writers find their first "careless rapture" has been snuffed out by middle

age, Dickens started the outstandingly successful *All The Year Round.* Incidentally, he was for a while editor of the *Daily News* as well. His physical energy was boundless. Mr. Wardle once suggested that his guests at Dingley Dell should take a twenty-mile walk to shake off the effects of that wedding breakfast and be ready to tuck in again when they came back. Dickens was just as capable of making the same kind of suggestion to his guests at Gad's Hill, the country home in Kent he had long desired and was at last able to acquire in 1856.

Dickens was always fascinated by the stage, and his best-loved diversion was amateur acting. He seemed to have no ambition to write plays himself; no doubt the inability of the actors to play the parts as Dickens heard them being played in his own head made playwriting utterly unworth his while. However, acting in other people's plays gave him great pleasure. He started an amateur company to raise funds for some artistic charity, which never came to anything. My grandmother, Emmeline Montague, who had retired from the stage when she was married, was Dickens's favorite amateur leading lady.

Then Dickens discovered that if he confined himself to the parts he had written in his own novels, he was one of the greatest actors that ever lived. Indeed, one can say with complete assurance that the composition of a Dickens novel was closer to acting than to writing. Perhaps if Dickens had not exhausted himself with those readings of his own works that he gave to enraptured audiences, he might have lived longer. But he was a happier man dying as he did than if he had lived on to write more novels and realize the slow ebbing of those tides that had once risen so high.

To me there is something distasteful in the spectacle of hyenas nosing in the entrails of dead lions. It adds nothing to Dickens's glory as a writer to point out when or where Ellen Ternan bore him a child. His decision to tell the world that he was going to be separated from the wife who had borne him ten children was his own affair. A genius is responsible only to

his own work for his behavior. In the case of a man like Dickens, whose impact on the public has never been surpassed, ordinary people cannot resist being gratified to discover that their idol can in certain circumstances behave with as much commonplace stupidity as themselves. The debunking of great men is as consoling to the ordinary man as a pat on the back. Dickens was essentially a man's man and really knew very little at all about the minds of women, however well he could paint their external features. All his young heroines are pretty dolls, and he lived during a period when, at any rate in England, most men were still hoping optimistically that women really were dolls.

Accepting the fact that Dickens contributed very little to our current way of dissecting character, I ask myself how much of this dissection is worthwhile, or

Uriah Heep

in other words, how much of it has added any significance to human nature that was unknown to Shakespeare? Dickens may be temporarily out of fashion with the avant-garde, but let us remember that Shakespeare was equally out of fashion with the avant-garde of the late seventeenth and early eighteenth centuries. It was an avant-garde at whom we smile tolerantly today as at the tricks of children. No doubt posterity will smile with equal tolerance at our avant-garde of today.

SARAJEVO

CONTINUED FROM PAGE 6

matic progress—went deep. The American anthropologist Lewis Morgan had sounded a note of self-confident hope for the entire age when he said, in 1877, "Democracy in government, brotherhood in society, equality in rights and privileges, and universal education, foreshadow the next higher plane of society to which experience, intelligence and knowledge are steadily tending." The emphasis here was on *steadily*: nothing could stop the onward march of mankind.

And the progress was very real. The age that died in 1914 was a brilliant one—so extravagant in its intellectual and aesthetic endowments that we who have come after can hardly believe in its reality. It was a comfortable age—for a considerable minority, at least—but it was more than a matter of Sunday walks in the Wienerwald, or country-house living, or a good five-cent cigar. It was an imposing age in the sciences, in the arts, even in forms of government. Men had done much and had risen high in the hundred years that came to an end that summer. From Napoleon's downfall in 1815 to the outbreak of war in 1914, the trend had been up.

"As happy as God in France," even the Germans used to say. For France these were the years of the *belle époque,* when all the world's artists came there to learn: Picasso and Juan Gris from Spain, Chagall and Archipenko from Russia, Piet Mondrian from the Netherlands, Brancusi from Romania, Man Ray and Max Weber from America, Modigliani from Italy. All made up the "School of Paris," a name which meant nothing but that in this Paris of the *avant-guerre* the world of the arts was at home.

"Paris drank the talents of the world," wrote the poet-impresario of those years, Guillaume Apollinaire. Debussy, Ravel, and Stravinsky composed music there. Nijinsky and Diaghilev were raising the modern ballet to new heights of brilliance and creativity. The year 1913 was, as Roger Shattuck puts it in *The Banquet Years,* the *annus mirabilis* of French literature: Proust's *Du Côté de chez Swann,* Alain-Fournier's *Le Grand Meaulnes,* Apollinaire's *Alcools,* Roger Martin du Gard's *Jean Barois,* Valéry Larbaud's *A. O. Barnabooth,* Péguy's *L'Argent,* Barrès's *La Colline inspirée,* and Colette's *L'Entrave* and *L'Envers du music-hall* appeared that year. "It is almost as if the war *had* to come in order to put an end to an extravaganza that could not have been sustained at this level." That was Paris.

Vienna was another great mongrel city that, like Paris, drank up talent—in this case the talents of a congeries of Austrians, Magyars, Czechs, Slovaks, Poles, Slovenes, Croats, Serbs, Jews, Turks, Transylvanians, and Gypsies. On Sunday mornings gentlemen strolled in the Prater ogling the cocottes; they rode the giant red Ferris wheel and looked out over the palaces and parks of the city; or they spent the morning at the coffeehouse, arguing pointlessly and interminably. It was a pleasure-loving city, but an intellectual one, too. The names of the men who walked Vienna's streets up to the eve of the war are stunning in their brilliance: Gustav Mahler, Sigmund Freud, Sandor Ferenczi, Ernst Mach, Béla Bartók, Rainer Maria Rilke, Franz Kafka, Robert Musil, Arthur Schnitzler, Hugo von Hofmannsthal, Richard Strauss, Stefan Zweig—these hardly begin to exhaust the list. (There were more sinister names, too. Adolf Hitler lived in Vienna between 1909 and 1913, an out-of-work, shabby *Bettgeher*—a daytime renter of other people's beds—absorbing the virulent anti-Semitism that charged the Viennese social atmosphere; so did Leon Trotsky, who spent his evenings listening contemptuously to the wranglings of the Social Democratic politicians at the Café Central.)

England was still gilded by the afterglow of the Edwardian Age: the British Empire straddled the earth, controlling more than a quarter of the surface of the globe. If the realities of trade had begun to shift, and if British industry and British naval supremacy were faced with a growing challenge from the United States and Hohenzollern Germany, the vast British overseas investments tended to hide the fact. England had its intellectual brilliance, too: these were the years of Hardy, Kipling, Shaw, Wells, the young D. H. Lawrence and the young Wyndham Lewis, Arnold Bennett, Gilbert Murray, A. E. Housman, H. H. Munro (Saki)—who would die in the war—and many others, like Rupert Brooke, Robert Graves, Siegfried Sassoon, and Wilfred Owen, who were as yet hardly known.

As for the Kaiser's Germany, it is melancholy to reflect that if Wilhelm II himself, that summer in 1914, had only waited—five years, ten years, or twenty—Germany might have had it all. But Wilhelm was shrewd, treacherous, and hysterical, a chronic bully whose mother had never loved him. His habitual style of discourse was the neurotic bluster of a small man who has had the bad luck to be called upon to stomp about in a giant's boots. Wilhelm II lived all his life in the shadow of "the Great Emperor," his grandfather Wilhelm I, who had created a united Greater Germany with the help of his brilliant chancellor, Prince Otto von Bismarck; he wanted to make the world stand in awe of him, but he did not know, precisely, how to go about it.

If only he could have been patient: Austria-Hungary was really a German satellite; the Balkans and the Middle East looked to Berlin; Germany's industrial hegemony on the continent was secure, and might soon have knocked Britain from her commanding place in the world's trade. By 1914, fourteen Germans had won Nobel Prizes in the sciences (by contrast, their nearest competitors, the French, had won only nine).

But the lesson is something more than a chapbook homily on patience. Wilhelm's personal anxiety merely expressed in microcosm the larger German anxiety about the nation's place in the world. Something strange lay beneath the stolid prosperity of the Hohenzollern Age—a surfeit with peace, a lust for violence, a belief in death, an ominous mystique of war. "Without war the world would quickly sink into materialism," the elder Von Moltke, chief of the German General Staff, had proclaimed in 1880; and he, his nephew the younger Von Moltke, and the caste of Prussian militarists they represented could presumably save the world from that tawdry fate. But this belief in war was not a monopoly of the Right: even Thomas Mann, spokesman of German humanism, could ask, in 1914, "Is not war a purification, a liberation, an enormous hope?" adding complacently, "Is not peace an element in civil corruption?"

There had been peace in the world for too long. From Berlin, in the spring of 1914, Colonel House wrote to Woodrow Wilson: "The whole of Germany is charged with electricity. Everybody's nerves are tense. It only requires a spark to set the whole thing off." People were saying: "Better a horrible ending than a horror without end." In expressing this spirit of violence and disorientation, Germany was merely precocious. It expressed a universal European malaise.

The malaise was evident everywhere—in the new cults of political violence; in the new philosophies of men like Freud, Nietzsche, and Pareto, who stressed the unconscious and the irrational, and who exposed the lying pretensions of middle-class values and conventions; and in the sense of doom that permeated the avant-garde arts of the prewar years. Typical of this spirit of rebellion was the manifesto set forth in 1910 by the Italian Futurist painters: it declared that "all forms of imitation should be held in contempt and that all forms of originality glorified; that we should rebel against the tyranny of the words 'harmony' and 'good taste' . . . ; that a clean sweep be made of all stale and threadbare subject matter in order to express the vortex of modern life—a life of steel, pride, fever, and speed . . ."

In England and France, as in Germany and Italy, the darker strain was there. When the war came, a glad Rupert Brooke intoned:

Now God be thanked Who has matched us with His hour.

A fever was over Paris as the spring of 1914 slipped into summer. Charles Péguy—Dreyfusard, Socialist, man of good will and reason, to his intellectual generation "the pure man"—had caught this other darker spirit as well. That spring he had written:

Heureux ceux qui sont morts dans les grandes batailles . . .
Happy are those who have died in great battles,
Lying on the ground before the face of God . . .

By September of that year he himself was dead.

No doubt we shall never understand it completely. What is absolutely clear about the outbreak of the First World War is that it was catastrophic: the hecatombs of dead, the appalling material waste, the destruction, and the pain of those four years tell us that. In our hearts we know that since that bootless, reckless, bloody adventure nothing has really come right again in the world. Democracy in government, brotherhood in society, equality in rights and privileges, universal education—all those evidences of "the next higher plane of society" to which experience, intelligence, and knowledge seemed to be steadily tending—gave way to mass conscription and the central direction of war, the anonymity of the trenches, the calculated propaganda lie: in short, between 1914 and 1918 Europe evolved many of the brutal features of the modern totalitarian state. And twenty-one years after the last shot was fired in the First World War, a second war came: a war of even greater brutality, moral degradation, and purposeful evil, but one where the issues at last matched the scale on which men had, a quarter-century earlier, blindly chosen to fight. Here was a deadly justice. That such a war should be fought at all was the direct outcome of the spiritual wasteland that the first war engendered.

Woodrow Wilson, greeting the Armistice, was able to proclaim to his fellow Americans that "everything" for which his countrymen had fought had been accomplished. He could assert that it was America's "fortunate duty to assist by example, by sober, friendly counsel, and by material aid in the establishment of a just democracy throughout the world."

But today we know that the poet Robert Graves more truly expressed the spirit of the nightmare from which the world awakened in 1918 when he wrote, "The news [of the Armistice] sent me out walking alone along the dyke above the marshes of Rhuddlan . . . cursing and sobbing and thinking of the dead."

Edmund Stillman is a writer with a special interest in southeastern Europe and the Middle East. He is the author of The Balkans *in the Life World Library, and co-author (with William Pfaff) of* The New Politics *and* The Politics of Hysteria.

PENELOPE
AND
THE POET

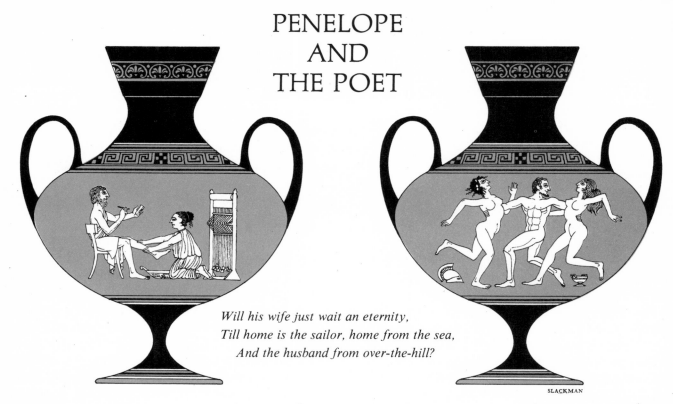

Will his wife just wait an eternity,
Till home is the sailor, home from the sea,
And the husband from over-the-hill?

SLACKMAN

Ulysses, as readers of the Odyssey *know, took an unconscionable time in getting back to Ithaca and his wife Penelope after the fall of Troy, and stopped off with a lot of girls on the way. Homer dealt with this protracted mustering-out and repatriation problem from a male viewpoint. In his account, dutiful, loyal Penelope just waits, coping with her unwanted suitors as best she can. How a woman of spirit might have felt about all this, what the actual home-coming might have been like, and how Homer gathered his facts—all this is the basis of a new comedy by a lively new playwright, Helen MacInnes, the author of such celebrated novels of mystery, politics, and suspense as* Assignment in Brittany, Above Suspicion, Decision at Delphi, *and the current best seller* The Venetian Affair.

Miss MacInnes, who in private life is the wife of Gilbert Highet, calls her play Home is the Hunter. *It will be published in late September by Harcourt, Brace and World.*

The fragment that follows comes from Act One, Scene Three. Penelope, though beset by Melas, Eryx, and other quarreling suitors, has secretly learned that Ulysses—alone and disguised as a beggar— is back on Ithaca, planning a way to destroy his well-armed rivals. Meanwhile his old nurse Clia, who is now Penelope's maid, announces a new arrival in this overcrowded house.

CLIA. (*She knocks on the bedroom door, opens it a little.*) Penelope! You've a visitor; he's traveled a long way to see you!

PENELOPE (*urgently*). Clia, don't tease me. Who is it?

CLIA (*to* HOMER). Poor dear! She's always thinking it might be Ulysses. (*to* PENELOPE) It's your friend the poet—the man who is making up the story about Ulysses. (*She leaves the bedroom door.*)

HOMER. Clia, I don't make up stories. . . . I describe the truth. That is why I am here in Ithaca now. If I didn't want to see the real facts for myself, I could stay in Smyrna where I like the climate. And

another thing—why do you call your master *Ulysses*? Give him his real name—Odysseus. Really, Clia . . . Ulysses! A complete bastardization. It won't even scan properly.

CLIA. Penelope always calls him Ulysses. She says Odysseus is too big a mouthful. For instance (*She points to Ulysses' chair.*), you can say "Ulysses' chair" without too much of a splutter. But who's going to take a deep enough breath to say "Odysseus's chair"?

HOMER (*stiffly*). I still say Odysseus.

CLIA (*placatingly*). Turned out a nice day, hasn't it? How far have you been traveling, this time?

HOMER. From Thessaly.

CLIA. Over all those mountains? My, that's quite a journey. . . . (*She strikes her forehead.*) Your cloak—your boots—I was so excited I forgot to welcome you properly. I'll just rush downstairs and get a basin of water. I'm sorry, I really am. . . .

HOMER (*smiling again*). What I need most is a drink. I've walked from the village, and I've collected as much dust in my throat as on my boots.

CLIA. Shan't be a moment. . . . (*She has moved quickly to the door as she speaks, and as* PENELOPE *opens the bedroom door and enters the sitting room,* CLIA *exclaims and rushes out.*)

PENELOPE. (*Coming forward to* HOMER *with hands outstretched. She has changed her dress—She is now wearing a blue silk gown, and her hair is charmingly arranged.*) *Homer*! How wonderful to see you! . . . And how well you look. (*She takes his cloak and places it on one of the chairs.*)

HOMER. You are looking remarkably well, yourself. (*He looks at her critically, though.*)

PENELOPE (*looking down at her dress*). You don't like it? I thought it was—quite—pretty.

HOMER. It's most charming, but isn't it a little—lighthearted? Not

BY HELEN MACINNES

quite what I had imagined you wearing.

PENELOPE. Really? (*She is amused.* HOMER *has been looking for a place to lay his harp. He almost puts it on Ulysses' chair, but then refrains.*) Yes, put it there.

HOMER. But it's your husband's chair, and only Odysseus sits there.

PENELOPE. Put it on the chair. Ulysses will be honored.

HOMER. My dear, I wish you'd call him Odysseus.

PENELOPE (*laughing*). But my tongue trips over it. (*She pulls two chairs forward, and invites him to sit down.*) You always amaze me. You've never been in this room before, yet you know all about Ulysses' chair.

HOMER. That's easily explained. People talk, you know. And poets listen.

PENELOPE. And when Homer sings, the people grow silent.

HOMER (*now in very good humor*). If there's one thing nicer than being treated to a compliment, it's having a pretty woman pay it.

PENELOPE. That wasn't a compliment; it was the truth. No poet is so . . . (*She breaks off as the door opens.* CLIA *comes in with a bronze basin of water and a folded towel over her arm.* AMARYLLIS *follows her, carrying a large silver goblet of wine.*) What's this? (PENELOPE *stares down at* HOMER's *boots and springs to her feet.*) Heavens! What have we done—or rather, what haven't we done? Clia, you know the rule of this house: no stranger, however poor, arrives at our door without being welcomed. And what is our welcome?

CLIA. To speak kindly and invite him to enter; to bathe his hands and feet; to offer him bread and wine and a warm corner by the hearth.

HOMER. Now, now, Penelope . . . I always think of you as the gentlest woman I've ever met. Besides, you didn't notice my boots either, did you?

PENELOPE. No. . . . (*She begins to laugh, too.*) All this excitement today is too much for me, I'm afraid. (*She draws* CLIA *aside, who has placed the basin before* HOMER *and now kneels at his feet.*) Let me. (*She kneels in front of* HOMER *and begins to draw off his boots.* CLIA, *now on her feet, places the towel over* PENELOPE's *shoulder, and then beckons* AMARYLLIS *forward.* HOMER *takes the goblet quickly, has a long drink, and then raises it with a sigh of pleasure.*)

HOMER. Oh, come bring to me a pint of wine, and pour it in a silver tassie!

PENELOPE. Tassie? What on earth is that?

HOMER. A word I've just invented. Sounds amusing in a foreign kind of way, doesn't it? Not as heavy as "goblet," not as solemn as "beaker." Of course, you could get rid of that cold solemnity and add a touch of the sun by saying—now, let me see. . . . Yes. . . . "Come bring to me a pint of wine, a beaker full of the warm south." Full of the warm south. . . . Yes, that stirs memories as well as one's palate. (*He nods, drinks, and sighs with pleasure as he slips his feet into the basin of water.*)

AMARYLLIS. South is south, and north is north. You can't pour either of them into a beaker! (*She smiles saucily and tosses her head.*)

HOMER (*noticing her with amusement*). Ah, my public! How sensitive, how percipient, how appreciative! No wonder poets can

starve to death.

CLIA (*warningly*). Amaryllis! This isn't Melas you're talking to. It's Homer, the poet.

AMARYLLIS (*unabashed*). He doesn't look as if he'll starve to death.

PENELOPE. Leave the room.

HOMER (*laughing*). I'm going to take that as a compliment, Amaryllis.

AMARYLLIS (*all smiles, as she strikes a pretty pose for* HOMER's *benefit*). If it's a compliment you want, I can do better than that.

PENELOPE (*flaring up*). If you don't leave this room at once, you'll leave this house. (AMARYLLIS *looks at her angrily; goes out.*)

HOMER. Now, I'm afraid that was my fault somehow. My dear Penelope, you're all on edge. This isn't like you.

PENELOPE. Isn't it? (*She bathes his feet for a moment, and then smiles.*) How much do you really know me, I wonder?

HOMER. You are one of the chief characters in my new poem. Of course I know you. Well. How else could I make you come alive? (PENELOPE *stares at him, and sits back on her heels, forgetting her duty.*) That was a pretty girl, all the same. Amaryllis, did you say? A sweet name for a sweet face.

CLIA. *And* an empty head.

HOMER. Amaryllis . . . Amaryllis. There's music in the name. To play with Amaryllis—to play with Amaryllis in the shade. No . . . to *sport* with Amaryllis in the shade or with the tangles of Niobe's hair. . . . (*He shakes his head.*) That isn't quite right. Niobe—she's too tragic. I'll have to think of someone else.

PENELOPE (*smiling, fascinated by* HOMER's *words, still sitting back on her heels*). To sport with Amaryllis . . . that sounds very appropriate to me. I'd keep that phrase, at least. Are you thinking of using it in the new poem? And the pint of wine, complete with tassie? . . . Oh, Clia! We're listening to poetry being made!

HOMER. I'll use the phrases—if I can remember them. That's the trouble, you know: there are too many phrases running through my head. It's difficult to get them all into my poems.

PENELOPE. Then for every line of poetry you sing, there may be three that we shall never hear?

HOMER (*cheerfully*). Sad, isn't it? That's why poets all go slightly crazy. Occupational disease. Now, what about this object? (*He lifts a foot to be dried, and brings* PENELOPE *back to her duty again.*) Poor old feet! They've carried me many a mile. Why don't you rebel, feet? There isn't another part of my body that would take such a pounding and not complain. . . . (*He speaks vaguely, as if listening and inventing.*) Oh—the moon shines bright on Mrs. Porter, and on her daughter; they wash their feet in soda water. (*He laughs.*) Don't think too much of that, do you, Penelope?

PENELOPE. Who's Mrs. Porter, and what's soda water? Or doesn't it matter when you're thinking up poetry? (*She laughs, too, as she finishes her task, and turns to* CLIA *for a pair of sandals.*) But, Homer, quite seriously, it *is* such a waste not to use all the lines you invent (HOMER *is setting "Mrs. Porter" to a catchy little tune.*)—even the silly ones.

HOMER. Waste? Why, I only plucked these words out of the air. If I don't use them, I send them back where they came from; and they'll hover around until another poet reaches up and catches them. There will always be plenty of poets. What I've lost, they'll find. So there's no waste. (*He bends to help* PENELOPE *fasten on the sandals. He touches* PENELOPE'S *head.*) Thank you. That was the sweetest welcome ever given me. (CLIA *has removed the basin and towel and dusty boots, and bustles from the room. He helps* PENELOPE *to rise.*)

PENELOPE. Why don't you tell your phrases to your pupils? They could always use them.

HOMER. I teach my pupils *how* to sing, but I'll never teach them *what* to sing. There's such a thing as integrity, you know, even in the literary world. Besides, some of my pupils are getting too big for their tunics. Why, someday, they will be claiming that they helped to compose the *Iliad.*

PENELOPE. I love the *Iliad.* I can hardly wait until your next poem comes out.

HOMER (*sharply*). And *when* did you hear the *Iliad*?

PENELOPE. Oh, we've had several wandering minstrels during the last few years. They stay overnight, and sing to us, and it's always something from the *Iliad.* They say it's at the top of the request list, wherever they go.

HOMER. Were they from my school in Smyrna?

PENELOPE. Some were pupils of your pupils, I think.

HOMER (*rising abruptly*). You see! . . . They'll be changing my lines, adding verses of their own! A hundred years from now, and I won't recognize some of my own poetry.

PENELOPE. A *hundred* years from *now*?

HOMER. What do you think I'm writing for? Only for the people who live today? Why, there's no reason for a good story to die. It can be passed down from mouth to mouth, from heart to heart, for at least a hundred years. Perhaps ten hundred.

PENELOPE. A thousand years? Oh, Homer, don't! The gods will hear you and be jealous.

HOMER (*looking up humorously*). All right, gods, I take that back. No thousand years, but just whatever time it pleases you. (*to* PENELOPE) Is that better?

PENELOPE (*shocked*). How can you talk that way? Aren't you afraid?

HOMER. I don't have to believe everything I sing about the gods, do I? If gods *are* godlike, then they are much too great to be flattered by the myths men create around them.

PENELOPE (*teasingly*). I thought everything you composed was based on fact.

HOMER. I tell the truth about men and this man-world. But when it comes to gods—well, Penelope, you can be realistic about the earth, but all you can do is speculate about Heaven.

PENELOPE. What are you going to call your new poem?

HOMER. The *Odyssey.* The adventures of Odysseus on his long voyage home. When I arrived here this morning, I hoped to find Odysseus and get certain facts from him. I've heard plenty of rumors, of course. . . .

PENELOPE (*grimly*). So have I.

HOMER. But I have reliable information that he has left Calypso and her island, and is homeward bound. He's practically here, Penelope!

PENELOPE. If he doesn't meet another Calypso.

HOMER. Penelope, that isn't like you to be jealous—after all, Odysseus had —

PENELOPE. trouble finding transportation. Yes, I've heard that one.

HOMER. Now, now, my dear—you've got to stop all this. You've got to start being Penelope again.

PENELOPE (*pathetically*). But I *am* being Penelope.

HOMER. I remember Penelope as the patient, faithful wife, who waits for her husband to return from the war. She understands, and to understand is to forgive.

PENELOPE. Is it?

HOMER (*ignoring that*). She is gentle, sweet, trusting, and kind. That's the Penelope I know. She's the sort of woman every man wants to come home to.

PENELOPE. And he'll get so bored with her that he'll run away again! Ulysses has had the taste of adventure, and of a woman like that— like that Calypso. Why, he spent *months* with her on that island!

HOMER. You are judging him before he can tell you what really happened. He may have been shipwrecked. He may have had to build another ship. He may have been ill. And it may have been the island's fault. It is perhaps a magic island—an island filled with noises, sounds and sweet airs, that give delight—and hurt not. (*He pauses for a second.*) Why! That's not bad, not bad at all. I'll try to remember that one. It isn't in my meter, though. Pity. . . . Ah, well . . . Penelope, haven't you ever dreamed of such an island? Most of us want a magic island, just now and again.

PENELOPE (*bursting into tears, and throwing herself on his breast*). Oh, Homer, I'm so miserable! (*He tries to comfort her, clasping her awkwardly.*) You don't know what it's like to wait and wait and wonder if your husband will ever come back to you. Or, when he does, if he still loves you.

HOMER. He loves you. He's coming home, isn't he?

PENELOPE (*drawing away, and in control of herself again*). Is he coming home because he loves me? Or is he tired of seeking the world and wouldn't it be nice to relax with quiet, sweet, gentle, kind Penelope for a while? That's not good enough!

HOMER. Penelope!

PENELOPE. You don't believe me? Oh, Homer, how blind you are! (*She begins to laugh.*)

HOMER (*sharply*). This is no laughing matter. Do you know what you're doing? You're ruining the *Odyssey.* (*He strides angrily to* PENELOPE'S *embroidery frame.*) Yes, I've composed one of the best passages I've ever done—about you, sitting here, day by day, weaving at your loom. And you took up embroidery, instead. Oh, I should never have made a poem about a woman.

PENELOPE (*subdued*). I didn't mean to ruin anything.

HOMER. You know I pride myself on the accuracy of my details— whether it's the wine-red sea at sunset; the mountain lion crouching on a jagged crag; or Helen, on the ramparts of Troy, walking in beauty like the night. . . . And *you* had to go and embroider!

PENELOPE (*helpfully*). But you could change . . .

HOMER. Change what I have composed? Not one word, not one image!

PENELOPE. Well—if anyone ever says you've been inaccurate about me, just blame it on your pupils who don't copy you correctly.

WHERE ART THOU, MUSE?

With all the science fiction produced in the past two hundred years, why hasn't there been at least a smattering of science verse?

"The subject, Sir, cannot be made poetical," was Dr. Johnson's damping comment about a contemporary who tried in a poem, "The Fleece," to describe scientific sheep farming. Some years later, Erasmus Darwin in "The Loves of the Plants" and "The Economy of Vegetation" tried to cross-pollinate botany with poetry. These went over like lead balloons. Another epic failure was "The Newtonian System," versified by a Fellow of the Royal Society; and if you look long enough in old bookstores, you may find a copy of Sarah Hoare's "Poems of Conchology." A pretty thin showing, the lot.

Yet there is no question that science poetry will be the next great breakthrough on the literary frontier.

Indeed, a little group of writers and scientists living in and around Cambridge, Massachusetts, has already organized to do the job. We have named our project *Scientific Poetry: Lyricism Applied To Technology*, or SPLATT; and we welcome all who seriously wish to advance the new art form. Our team is presently made up of four writers and two scientists. We know we aren't going to set the Charles on fire, but after only five meetings we have already produced our first fruit, a Shakespearean sonnet on the Second Law of Thermodynamics.

It hasn't been easy. Our first meeting was marred by bickering and jockeying for status, like an acting out of C. P. Snow's *Two Cultures and the Scientific Revolution*, but we are moving forward. Here are excerpts from the minutes of the initial SPLATT meetings:

May 8. Opening session at the home of Dr. B., attended by sixteen writers and twelve scientists. Dearth of science verse discussed. Ancient poets cited as scientists of their day—Lucretius's *De Rerum Natura* (forerunner of atomic theory), Virgil's *Georgics* on the subject of scientific manuring, etc. Refreshments were served. All present were asked to bring ideas to next meeting.

May 15. Many members absent, but a nucleus of ten proceeded with the meeting. Miss C. told of Shelley's devotion to science, quoting Alfred North Whitehead: "What the hills were to the youth of Wordsworth, a chemical laboratory was to Shelley. . . . Physical experiments guide his imagery. For example, the Earth's exclamation [in *Prometheus Unbound*] 'The vaporous exultation not to be confined!' is the poetic transcript of 'the expansive force of gases,' as it is termed in books on science. . . ."

Prof. G. said this shows there need not be any hard dichotomy between poet and scientist, and the whimsical bit that goes

> Poet: *"O Cuckoo, shall I call thee bird*
> *Or but a wandering voice?"*
> Scientist: *"Mark X against the one preferred;*
> *Give reasons for your choice"*

is grossly misleading.

Members were asked to select a theme for the first SPLATT verse. The following were offered and eliminated for one reason or another: Botulism in Food Fishes, Functional Calculus of First-Order Identities, Cybernetics, Stress-Strain in Precast Concrete. The theme finally agreed upon is the Second Law of Thermodynamics. The sonnet form has been selected as having the highest reliability factor. Next meeting will program the input.

May 29. Five members present. The Second Law of Thermodynamics defined as dealing with dissipation of energy; i.e., *it is impossible to construct an engine operating in cycle whose only effect is to transfer heat from one body to another at a higher temperature.* Simply stated, heat will not pass automatically from a cooler body to a hotter body. We will attempt to translate this into human values and insights—as great poetry must do with any theme—while at the same time satisfying the scientific mind. (Mr. G. offered a mathematical formula explaining the Second Law. It did not scan.) The committee on materials analysis suggested that since most sonnets are about Love, our subject with its warm and cooler bodies had possibilities for a kind of contrast structurization; e.g., the power of love to stoke up and incandesce a cooler element by heat transfer versus the impossibility of this happening in thermodynamics. Our Shakespearean expert, Mr. W. H., took up the idea, and we evolved the following opening lines:

> *Two hearts, one cool, one ardent, when they meet*
> *May work an alchemy of wondrous force . . .*

We have a feeling of elation. We are off the ground at last!

From these few excerpts you can see the work involved, the problems in creativity that had to be overcome by really inspired teamwork. Here is our completed sonnet:

> *Two hearts, one cool, one ardent, when they meet*
> *May work an alchemy of wondrous force:*
> *The warmer, pulsing with augmented heat*
> *Returns the flow to warm its cooler source.*
> *No man-made instrument can thus perform!*
> *Ingenious though it be, and free of flaw,*
> *The mightiest engine must obey the norm*
> *Of Thermodynamism's Second Law:*
> *Heat cannot be reversed. By slow degrees*
> *It wanes each time the action is replayed,*
> *The villain Friction drains its energies*
> *And by its own device the plot's betrayed;*
> *The Law emerges evermore the hero*
> *So long as $\int \frac{T - To}{T} \, dQ = O.$*

By MAURICE SAGOFF

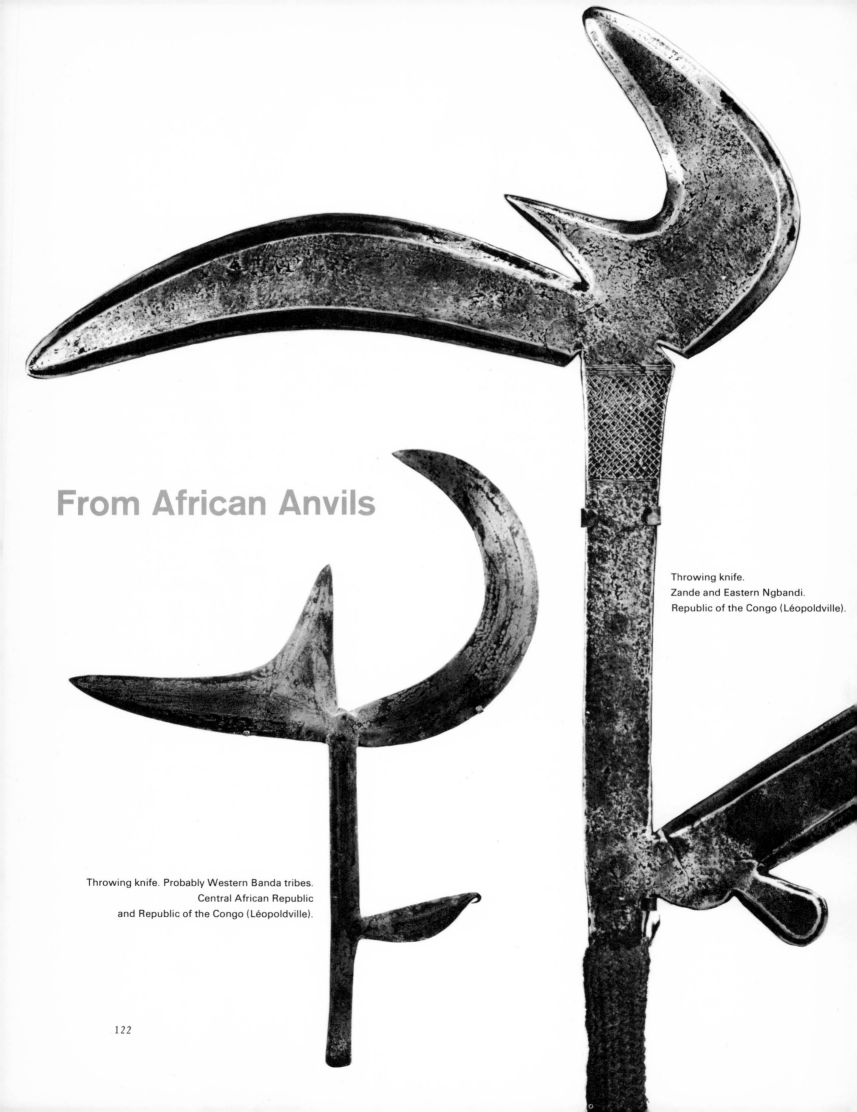

From African Anvils

Throwing knife.
Zande and Eastern Ngbandi.
Republic of the Congo (Léopoldville).

Throwing knife. Probably Western Banda tribes.
Central African Republic
and Republic of the Congo (Léopoldville).

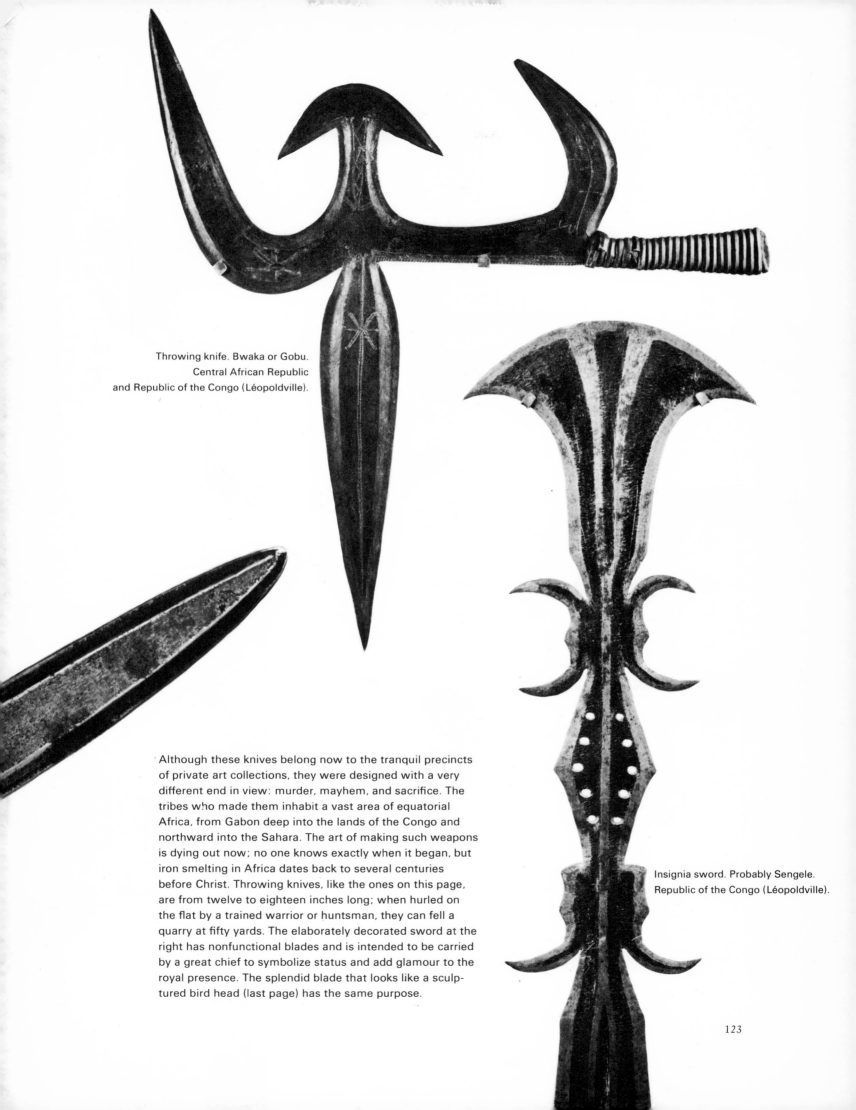

Throwing knife. Bwaka or Gobu.
Central African Republic
and Republic of the Congo (Léopoldville).

Although these knives belong now to the tranquil precincts
of private art collections, they were designed with a very
different end in view: murder, mayhem, and sacrifice. The
tribes who made them inhabit a vast area of equatorial
Africa, from Gabon deep into the lands of the Congo and
northward into the Sahara. The art of making such weapons
is dying out now; no one knows exactly when it began, but
iron smelting in Africa dates back to several centuries
before Christ. Throwing knives, like the ones on this page,
are from twelve to eighteen inches long; when hurled on
the flat by a trained warrior or huntsman, they can fell a
quarry at fifty yards. The elaborately decorated sword at the
right has nonfunctional blades and is intended to be carried
by a great chief to symbolize status and add glamour to the
royal presence. The splendid blade that looks like a sculp-
tured bird head (last page) has the same purpose.

Insignia sword. Probably Sengele.
Republic of the Congo (Léopoldville).

123

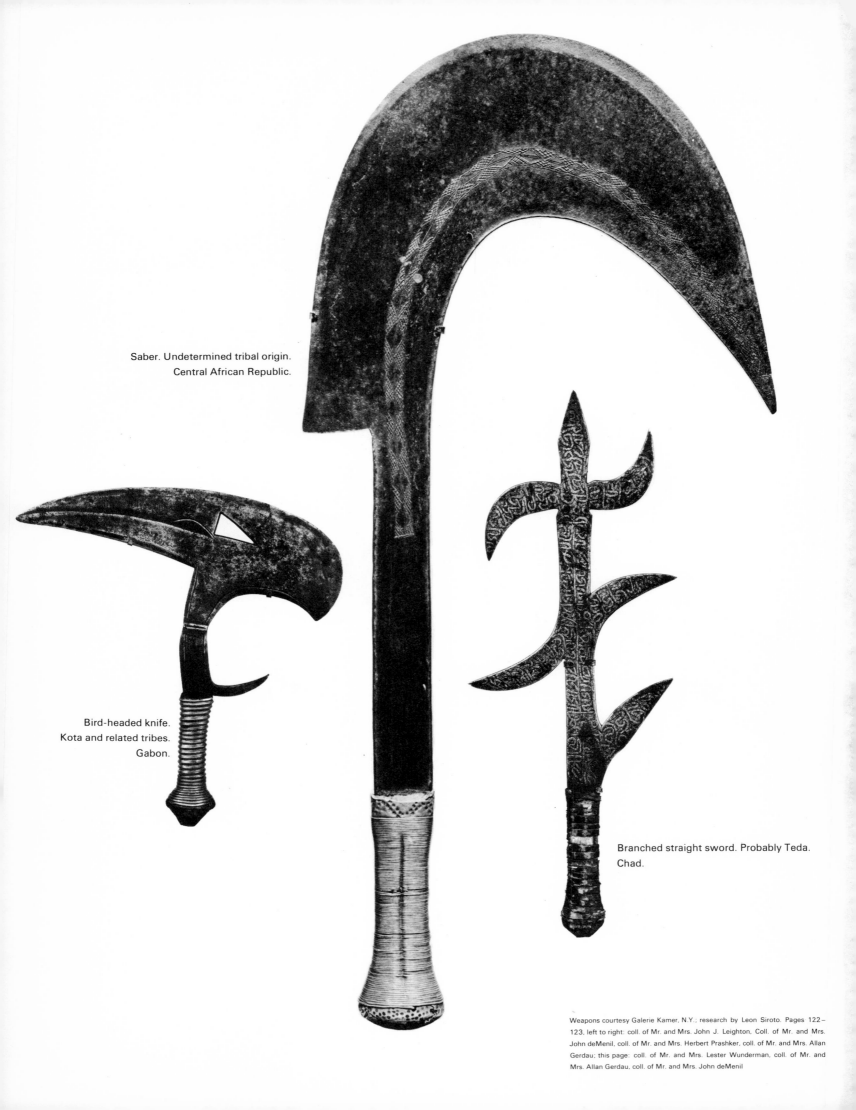

Saber. Undetermined tribal origin.
Central African Republic.

Bird-headed knife.
Kota and related tribes.
Gabon.

Branched straight sword. Probably Teda.
Chad.

Weapons courtesy Galerie Kamer, N.Y.; research by Leon Siroto. Pages 122–123, left to right: coll. of Mr. and Mrs. John J. Leighton, Coll. of Mr. and Mrs. John deMenil, coll. of Mr. and Mrs. Herbert Prashker, coll. of Mr. and Mrs. Allan Gerdau; this page: coll. of Mr. and Mrs. Lester Wunderman, coll. of Mr. and Mrs. Allan Gerdau, coll. of Mr. and Mrs. John deMenil